CRIME NEVER PAYS

'Murder most foul' – the first and the oldest crime. Stories about murder, in poem, play, and novel, have been with us for a long time. They held audiences spell-bound in the theatres of ancient Greece; they hold audiences today glued to their television sets. Readers engrossed in the pages of the latest murder mystery sit up reading half the night, in order to find out 'whodunnit'.

Murder stories continue to fascinate, appal, shock, and the genre today is wide-ranging. There are the classic detective stories, where the murderer's wits are pitted against the forces of law and order. We struggle with the detective to pick up the clues and to draw tight the net of justice around the criminal. There are the dramas in lawcourts when the murderer is brought to trial; the tales of ordinary people leading ordinary lives, pitchforked into tragedy by the unexpected eruption of some murderous passion. There are the stories where we see the world through the murderer's eyes, distorted and blurred by obsession, hate, jealousy, greed, madness . . .

This collection of murder stories offers a taste of many styles: puzzling, chilling, bizarre, horrifying. Let us join one of the characters in Agatha Christie's story:

'I feel,' said Jane dreamily, 'that I would like to wallow in crime this evening.'

OXFORD BOOKWORMS COLLECTION

Acknowledgements

The editors and publishers are grateful for permission to use the following copyright material:

'Three is a Lucky Number' from *The Allingham Case Book* by MARGERY ALLINGHAM, published by Chatto & Windus. © P. & M. Youngman Carter 1969. Reprinted by permission of Curtis Brown Group Ltd.

'The Companion' by AGATHA CHRISTIE taken from the collection *The Thirteen Problems*. Copyright © Agatha Christie Mallowan 1932. Reprinted by permission of Aitken & Stone Ltd.

'The Case for the Defence' from *Collected Stories* by GRAHAM GREENE, published by William Heinemann Ltd and The Bodley Head Ltd. Reprinted by permission of Laurence Pollinger Ltd.

'Sauce for the Goose' from *Chillers* by PATRICIA HIGHSMITH (first published under the title 'Home Bodies' in *Ellery Queen's Mystery Magazine*, 1972). All rights reserved. © 1972 by Patricia Highsmith. Reprinted by kind permission of the author.

'Ricochet' by ANGELA NOEL from *London Mystery Selection No. 124*, March 1980. Reprinted by kind permission of the author.

'A Glowing Future' from *The Fever Tree and other stories* by RUTH RENDELL, published by Hutchinson. Reprinted by permission of Random Century Group Ltd and Peters Fraser & Dunlop Group Ltd.

'The Fountain Plays' from *Hangman's Holiday* by DOROTHY L. SAYERS, published by Victor Gollancz Ltd and Hodder & Stoughton. Reprinted by permission of David Higham Associates Ltd.

CRIME NEVER PAYS

Short Stories

EDITED BY
Clare West

SERIES ADVISERS
H.G. Widdowson
Jennifer Bassett

OXFORD UNIVERSITY PRESS

Oxford University Press
Great Clarendon Street, Oxford OX2 6DP

Oxford New York
Athens Auckland Bangkok Bogota Bombay
Buenos Aires Calcutta Cape Town Dar es Salaam Delhi
Florence Hong Kong Istanbul Karachi Kuala Lumpur
Madras Madrid Melbourne Mexico City Nairobi
Paris Singapore Taipei Tokyo Toronto

and associated companies in
Berlin Ibadan

OXFORD and OXFORD ENGLISH
are trade marks of Oxford University Press

ISBN 0 19 422693 X

This edition © Oxford University Press 1993

First published 1993
Sixth impression 1996

No unauthorized photocopying

Typeset by Wyvern Typesetting Ltd, Bristol
Printed in England by Clays Ltd, St Ives plc

OXFORD BOOKWORMS
⁓ COLLECTION ⁓

FOREWORD

Texts of all kinds, including literary texts, are used as data for language teaching. They are designed or adapted and pressed into service to exemplify the language and provide practice in reading. These are commendable pedagogic purposes. They are not, however, what authors or readers of texts usually have in mind. The reason we read something is because we feel the writer has something of interest or significance to say and we only attend to the language to the extent that it helps us to understand what that might be. An important part of language learning is knowing how to adopt this normal reader role, how to use language to achieve meanings of significance to us, and so make texts our own.

The purpose of the *Oxford Bookworms Collection* is to encourage students of English to adopt this role. It offers samples of English language fiction, unabridged and unsimplified, which have been selected and presented to induce enjoyment, and to develop a sensitivity to the language through an appreciation of the literature. The intention is to stimulate students to find in fiction what Jane Austen found: 'the most thorough knowledge of human nature, the happiest delineation of its varieties, the liveliest effusions of wit and humour ... conveyed to the world in the best chosen language.' (*Northanger Abbey*)

H.G. Widdowson
Series Adviser

OXFORD BOOKWORMS
～ COLLECTION ～

None of the texts has been abridged or simplified in any way, but each volume contains notes and questions to help students in their understanding and appreciation.

Before each story
- a short biographical note on the author
- an introduction to the theme and characters of the story

After each story
- *Notes* Some words and phrases in the texts are marked with an asterisk*, and explanations for these are given in the notes. The expressions selected are usually cultural references or archaic and dialect words unlikely to be found in dictionaries. Other difficult words are not explained. This is because to do so might be to focus attention too much on the analysis of particular meanings, and to disrupt the natural reading process. Students should be encouraged by their engagement with the story to infer general and relevant meaning from context.
- *Discussion* These are questions on the story's theme and characters, designed to stimulate class discussion or to encourage the individual reader to think about the story from different points of view.
- *Language Focus* These questions and tasks direct the reader's attention to particular features of language use or style.
- *Activities* These are suggestions for creative writing activities, to encourage readers to explore or develop the ideas and themes of the story in various imaginative ways.
- *Ideas for Comparison Activities* These are occasional additional sections with ideas for discussion or writing, which compare and contrast a number of stories in the volume.

CURRENT TITLES

From the Cradle to the Grave
Short stories by Saki, Evelyn Waugh, Somerset Maugham, Roald Dahl, Frank Sargeson, Raymond Carver, H.E. Bates, Susan Hill
Crime Never Pays
Short stories by Agatha Christie, Graham Greene, Ruth Rendell, Angela Noel, Dorothy L. Sayers, Margery Allingham, Arthur Conan Doyle, Patricia Highsmith

Contents

THE COMPANION

THE AUTHOR

Agatha Christie was born in 1890. She wrote over seventy detective novels, more than a hundred short stories, and many stage plays. Her play *The Mousetrap* has been running in London since 1952. Many of her novels feature the Belgian detective, Hercule Poirot, or the elderly village lady, Miss Jane Marple. Among her best-known titles are *The Mysterious Affair at Styles, The Murder of Roger Ackroyd, Death on the Nile, Murder at the Vicarage*, and *Murder on the Orient Express*, which was made into a film in 1975. Because of the ingenuity and unfailing suspense of her plots she has remained one of the most popular detective writers of all time. She died in 1976.

THE STORY

Miss Marple is one of the famous characters of detective fiction. She is a small elderly lady, with quiet pleasant manners, who is fond of knitting; very far from being a great detective, you would think. But Miss Marple is a good listener. She has a very sharp eye for detail and a shrewd understanding of human nature. Many murderers have had cause to regret her interest in their affairs.

In this story Miss Marple is at a dinner party, listening to the tale of a crime told by a friend. The guests try to solve the mystery in Dr Lloyd's story, but it isn't even clear if a crime has been committed. Dr Lloyd describes two middle-aged ladies on holiday in Grand Canary; one of them drowns while swimming. A sad accident, it seems. Miss Marple listens carefully . . .

THE COMPANION

'Now, Dr Lloyd,' said Miss Helier. 'Don't *you* know any creepy stories?'

She smiled at him – the smile that nightly bewitched the theatre-going public. Jane Helier was sometimes called the most beautiful woman in England, and jealous members of her own profession were in the habit of saying to each other: 'Of course Jane's not an *artist*. She can't *act* – if you know what I mean. It's those eyes!'

And those 'eyes' were at this minute fixed appealingly on the grizzled elderly bachelor doctor who, for the last five years, had ministered to the ailments of the village of St Mary Mead.

With an unconscious gesture, the doctor pulled down his waistcoat (inclined of late to be uncomfortably tight) and racked his brains hastily, so as not to disappoint the lovely creature who addressed him so confidently.

'I feel,' said Jane dreamily, 'that I would like to wallow in crime this evening.'

'Splendid,' said Colonel Bantry, her host. 'Splendid, splendid.' And he laughed a loud hearty military laugh. 'Eh, Dolly?'

His wife, hastily recalled to the exigencies of social life (she had been planning her spring border) agreed enthusiastically.

'Of course it's splendid,' she said heartily but vaguely. 'I always thought so.'

'Did you, my dear?' said old Miss Marple, and her eyes twinkled a little.

'We don't get much in the creepy line – and still less in the criminal line – in St Mary Mead, you know, Miss Helier,' said Dr Lloyd.

'You surprise me,' said Sir Henry Clithering. The

ex-Commissioner of Scotland Yard* turned to Miss Marple. 'I always understood from our friend here that St Mary Mead is a positive hotbed of crime and vice.'

'Oh, Sir Henry!' protested Miss Marple, a spot of colour coming into her cheeks. 'I'm sure I never said anything of the kind. The only thing I ever said was that human nature is much the same in a village as anywhere else, only one has opportunities and leisure for seeing it at closer quarters.'

'But *you* haven't always lived here,' said Jane Helier, still addressing the doctor. 'You've been in all sorts of queer places all over the world – places where things *happen*!'

'That is so, of course,' said Dr Lloyd, still thinking desperately. 'Yes, of course ... Yes ... Ah! I have it!'

He sank back with a sigh of relief.

'It is some years ago now – I had almost forgotten. But the facts were really very strange – very strange indeed. And the final coincidence which put the clue into my hand was strange also.'

Miss Helier drew her chair a little nearer to him, applied some lipstick and waited expectantly. The others also turned interested faces towards him.

'I don't know whether any of you know the Canary Islands,' began the doctor.

'They must be wonderful,' said Jane Helier. 'They're in the South Seas, aren't they? Or is it the Mediterranean?'

'I've called in there on my way to South Africa,' said the Colonel. 'The Peak of Tenerife is a fine sight with the setting sun on it.'

'The incident I am describing happened in the island of Grand Canary, not Tenerife. It is a good many years ago now. I had had a breakdown in health and was forced to give up my practice in England and go abroad. I practised in Las Palmas, which is the principal town of Grand Canary. In many ways I enjoyed the life out there very much. The climate was mild and sunny, there was excellent surf bathing (and I am an enthusiastic bather) and the sea life of the port attracted me. Ships from all over the world put in at Las Palmas. I used to walk along the mole every morning far more interested than any member of the fair sex could be in a street of hat shops.

'As I say, ships from all over the world put in at Las Palmas. Sometimes they stay a few hours, sometimes a day or two. In the principal hotel there, the Metropole, you will see people of all races and nationalities – birds of passage. Even the people going to Tenerife usually come here and stay a few days before crossing to the other island.

'My story begins there, in the Metropole Hotel, one Thursday evening in January. There was a dance going on and I and a friend had been sitting at a small table watching the scene. There were a fair sprinkling of English and other nationalities, but the majority of the dancers were Spanish; and when the orchestra struck up a tango, only half a dozen couples of the latter nationality took the floor. They all danced well and we looked on and admired. One woman in particular excited our lively admiration. Tall, beautiful and sinuous, she moved with the grace of a half-tamed leopardess. There was something dangerous about her. I said as much to my friend and he agreed.

' "Women like that," he said, "are bound to have a history. Life will not pass them by."

' "Beauty is perhaps a dangerous possession," I said.

' "It's not only beauty," he insisted. "There is something else. Look at her again. Things are bound to happen to that woman, or because of her. As I said, life will not pass her by. Strange and exciting events will surround her. You've only got to look at her to know it."

'He paused and then added with a smile:

' "Just as you've only got to look at those two women over

there, and know that nothing out of the way could ever happen to either of them! They are made for a safe and uneventful existence."

'I followed his eyes. The two women he referred to were travellers who had just arrived – a Holland Lloyd boat had put into port that evening, and the passengers were just beginning to arrive.

'As I looked at them I saw at once what my friend meant. They were two English ladies – the thoroughly nice travelling English that you do find abroad. Their ages, I should say, were round about forty. One was fair and a little – just a little – too plump; the other was dark and a little – again just a little – inclined to scragginess. They were what is called well-preserved, quietly and inconspicuously dressed in well-cut tweeds, and innocent of any kind of make-up. They had that air of quiet assurance which is the birthright of well-bred Englishwomen. There was nothing remarkable about either of them. They were like thousands of their sisters. They would doubtless see what they wished to see, assisted by Baedeker*, and be blind to everything else. They would use the English library and attend the English Church in any place they happened to be, and it was quite likely that one or both of them sketched a little. And as my friend said, nothing exciting or remarkable would ever happen to either of them, though they might quite likely travel half over the world. I looked from them back to our sinuous Spanish woman with her half-closed smouldering eyes and I smiled.'

'Poor things,' said Jane Helier with a sigh. 'But I do think it's so silly of people not to make the most of themselves. That woman in Bond Street* – Valentine – is really wonderful. Audrey Denman goes to her; and have you seen her in "The Downward Step?" As the schoolgirl in the first act she's really marvellous. And yet Audrey is fifty if she's a day. As a matter of fact I happen to know she's really nearer sixty.'

'Go on,' said Mrs Bantry to Dr Lloyd. 'I love stories about

sinuous Spanish dancers. It makes me forget how old and fat I am.'

'I'm sorry,' said Dr Lloyd apologetically. 'But you see, as a matter of fact, this story isn't about the Spanish woman.'

'It isn't?'

'No. As it happens my friend and I were wrong. Nothing in the least exciting happened to the Spanish beauty. She married a clerk in a shipping office, and by the time I left the island she had had five children and was getting very fat.'

'Just like that girl of Israel Peters,' commented Miss Marple. 'The one who went on the stage and had such good legs that they made her principal boy in the pantomime*. Everyone said she'd come to no good, but she married a commercial traveller and settled down splendidly.'

'The village parallel,' murmured Sir Henry softly.

'No,' went on the doctor. 'My story is about the two English ladies.'

'Something happened to them?' breathed Miss Helier.

'Something happened to them – and the very next day, too.'

'Yes?' said Mrs Bantry encouragingly.

'Just for curiosity, as I went out that evening I glanced at the hotel register. I found the names easily enough. Miss Mary Barton and Miss Amy Durrant of Little Paddocks, Caughton Weir, Bucks. I little thought then how soon I was to encounter the owners of those names again – and under what tragic circumstances.

'The following day I had arranged to go for a picnic with some friends. We were to motor across the island, taking our lunch, to a place called (as far as I remember – it is so long ago) Las Nieves, a well-sheltered bay where we could bathe if we felt inclined. This programme we duly carried out, except that we were somewhat late in starting, so that we stopped on the way and picnicked, going on to Las Nieves afterwards for a bathe before tea.

'As we approached the beach, we were at once aware of a tremendous commotion. The whole population of the small village seemed to be gathered on the shore. As soon as they saw us they rushed towards the car and began explaining excitedly. Our Spanish not being very good, it took me a few minutes to understand, but at last I got it.

'Two of the mad English ladies had gone in to bathe, and one had swum out too far and got into difficulties. The other had gone after her and had tried to bring her in, but her strength in turn had failed and she too would have drowned had not a man rowed out in a boat and brought in rescuer and rescued – the latter beyond help.

'As soon as I got the hang of things I pushed the crowd aside and hurried down the beach. I did not at first recognize the two women. The plump figure in the black stockinet costume and the tight green rubber bathing cap awoke no chord of recognition as she looked up anxiously. She was kneeling beside the body of her friend, making somewhat amateurish attempts at artificial respiration. When I told her that I was a doctor she gave a sigh of relief, and I ordered her off at once to one of the cottages for a rub down and dry clothing. One of the ladies in my party went with her. I myself worked unavailingly on the body of the drowned woman in vain. Life was only too clearly extinct, and in the end I had reluctantly to give in.

'I rejoined the others in the small fisherman's cottage and there I had to break the sad news. The survivor was attired now in her own clothes, and I immediately recognized her as one of the two arrivals of the night before. She received the sad news fairly calmly, and it was evidently the horror of the whole thing that struck her more than any great personal feeling.

' "Poor Amy," she said. "Poor, poor Amy. She had been looking forward to the bathing here so much. And she was a good swimmer too. I can't understand it. What do you think it can have been, doctor?"

' "Possibly cramp. Will you tell me exactly what happened?"

' "We had both been swimming about for some time – twenty minutes I should say. Then I thought I would go in, but Amy said she was going to swim out once more. She did so, and suddenly I heard her call and realized she was crying for help. I swam out as fast as I could. She was still afloat when I got to her, but she clutched at me wildly and we both went under. If it hadn't been for that man coming out with his boat I should have been drowned too."

' "That has happened fairly often," I said. "To save anyone from drowning is not an easy affair."

' "It seems so awful," continued Miss Barton. "We only arrived yesterday, and were so delighting in the sunshine and our little holiday. And now this – this terrible tragedy occurs."

'I asked her then for particulars about the dead woman, explaining that I would do everything I could for her, but that the Spanish authorities would require full information. This she gave me readily enough.

'The dead woman, Miss Amy Durrant, was her companion and had come to her about five months previously. They had got on very well together, but Miss Durrant had spoken very little about her people. She had been left an orphan at an early age and had been brought up by an uncle and had earned her own living since she was twenty-one.

'And so that was that,' went on the doctor. He paused and said again, but this time with a certain finality in his voice, 'And so that was that.'

'I don't understand,' said Jane Helier. 'Is that all? I mean, it's very tragic, I suppose, but it isn't – well, it isn't what I call *creepy*.'

'I think there's more to follow,' said Sir Henry.

'Yes,' said Dr Lloyd, 'there's more to follow. You see, right at the time there was one queer thing. Of course I asked questions of the fishermen, etc., as to what they'd seen. They were eye-witnesses. And one woman had rather a funny story. I didn't pay any attention to it at the time, but it came back to me afterwards. She insisted, you see, that Miss Durrant wasn't in difficulties when she called out. The other swam out to her and according to this woman, deliberately held Miss Durrant's head under water. I didn't, as I say, pay much attention. It was such a fantastic story, and these things look so differently from the shore. Miss Barton might have tried to make her friend lose consciousness, realizing that the latter's panic-stricken clutching would drown them both. You see, according to the Spanish woman's story, it looked as though – well, as though Miss Barton was deliberately trying to drown her companion.

'As I say, I paid very little attention to this story at the time. It came back to me later. Our great difficulty was to find out anything about this woman, Amy Durrant. She didn't seem to have any relations. Miss Barton and I went through her things together. We found one address and wrote there, but it proved to be simply a room she had taken in which to keep her things. The landlady knew nothing, had only seen her when she took the room. Miss Durrant had remarked at the time that she always liked to have one place she could call her own to which she could return at any moment. There were one or two nice pieces of old furniture and some bound numbers of Academy pictures, and a trunk full of pieces of material bought at sales, but no personal belongings. She had mentioned to the landlady that her father and mother had died in India when she was a child and that she had been brought up by an uncle who was a clergyman, but she did not say if he was her father's or her mother's brother, so the name was no guide.

'It wasn't exactly mysterious, it was just unsatisfactory. There

When
Ms Amy
at hotel

must be many lonely women, proud and reticent, in just that position. There were a couple of photographs amongst her belongings in Las Palmas – rather old and faded and they had been cut to fit the frames they were in, so that there was no photographer's name upon them, and there was an old daguerreotype which might have been her mother or more probably her grandmother.

'Miss Barton had had two references with her. One she had forgotten, the other name she recollected after an effort. It proved to be that of a lady who was now abroad, having gone to Australia. She was written to. Her answer, of course, was a long time in coming, and I may say that when it did arrive there was no particular help to be gained from it. She said Miss Durrant had been with her as companion and had been most efficient and that she was a very charming woman, but that she knew nothing of her private affairs or relations.

'So there it was – as I say, nothing unusual, really. It was just the two things together that aroused my uneasiness. This Amy Durrant of whom no one knew anything, and the Spanish woman's queer story. Yes, and I'll add a third thing: When I was first bending over the body and Miss Barton was walking away towards the huts, she looked back. Looked back with an expression on her face that I can only describe as one of poignant anxiety – a kind of anguished uncertainty that imprinted itself on my brain.

'It didn't strike me as anything unusual at the time. I put it down to her terrible distress over her friend. But, you see, later I realized that they weren't on those terms. There was no devoted attachment between them, no terrible grief. Miss Barton was fond of Amy Durrant and shocked by her death – that was all.

'But, then, why that terrible poignant anxiety? That was the question that kept coming back to me. I had not been mistaken

worry

in that look. And almost against my will, an answer began to shape itself in my mind. Supposing the Spanish woman's story were true; supposing that Mary Barton wilfully and in cold blood tried to drown Amy Durrant. She succeeds in holding her under water whilst pretending to be saving her. She is rescued by a boat. They are on a lonely beach far from anywhere. And then I appear – the last thing she expects. A doctor! And an English doctor! She knows well enough that people who have been under water far longer than Amy Durrant have been revived by artificial respiration. But she has to play her part – to go off leaving me alone with her victim. And as she turns for one last look, a terrible poignant anxiety shows on her face. Will Amy Durrant come back to life *and tell what she knows?*'

'Oh!' said Jane Helier. 'I'm thrilled now.'

'Viewed in that aspect the whole business seemed more sinister, and the personality of Amy Durrant became more mysterious. Who was Amy Durrant? Why should she, an insignificant paid companion, be murdered by her employer? What story lay behind that fatal bathing expedition? She had entered Mary Barton's employment only a few months before. Mary Barton had brought her abroad, and the very day after they landed the tragedy had occurred. And they were both nice, commonplace, refined Englishwomen! The whole thing was fantastic and I told myself so. I had been letting my imagination run away with me.'

'You didn't do anything then?' asked Miss Helier.

'My dear young lady, what could I do? There was no evidence. The majority of the eye-witnesses told the same story as Miss Barton. I had built up my own suspicions out of a fleeting expression which I might possibly have imagined. The only thing I could and did do was to see that the widest inquiries were made for the relations of Amy Durrant. The next time I was in England I even went and saw the landlady of her room, with the results I have told you.'

'But you felt there was something wrong,' said Miss Marple.

Dr Lloyd nodded.

'Half the time I was ashamed of myself for thinking so. Who was I to go suspecting this nice, pleasant-mannered English lady of a foul and cold-blooded crime? I did my best to be as cordial as possible to her during the short time she stayed on the island. I helped her with the Spanish authorities. I did everything I could do as an Englishman to help a compatriot in a foreign country; and yet I am convinced that she knew I suspected and disliked her.'

'How long did she stay out there?' asked Miss Marple.

'I think it was about a fortnight. Miss Durrant was buried there, and it must have been about ten days later when she took a boat back to England. The shock had upset her so much that she felt she couldn't spend the winter there as she had planned. That's what she said.'

'Did it seem to have upset her?' asked Miss Marple.

The doctor hesitated.

'Well, I don't know that it affected her appearance at all,' he said cautiously.

'She didn't, for instance, grow fatter?' asked Miss Marple.

'Do you know – it's a curious thing your saying that. Now I come to think back, I believe you're right. She – yes, she did seem, if anything, to be putting on weight.'

'How horrible,' said Jane Helier with a shudder. 'It's like – it's like fattening on your victim's blood.'

'And yet, in another way, I may be doing her an injustice,' went on Dr Lloyd. 'She certainly said something before she left, which pointed in an entirely different direction. There may be, I think there are, consciences which work very slowly – which take some time to awaken to the enormity of the deed committed.

'It was the evening before her departure from the Canaries. She had asked me to go and see her, and had thanked me very warmly for all I had done to help her. I, of course, made light of the matter, said I had only done what was natural under the circumstances, and so on. There was a pause after that, and then she suddenly asked me a question.

' "Do you think," she asked, "that one is ever justified in taking the law into one's own hands?"

'I replied that that was rather a difficult question, but that on the whole, I thought not. The law was the law, and we had to abide by it.

' "Even when it is powerless?"

' "I don't quite understand."

' "It's difficult to explain; but one might do something that is considered definitely wrong – that is considered a crime, even, for a good and sufficient reason."

'I replied drily that possibly several criminals had thought that in their time, and she shrank back.

' "But that's horrible," she murmured. "Horrible."

'And then with a change of tone she asked me to give her something to make her sleep. She had not been able to sleep properly since – she hesitated – since that terrible shock.

' "You're sure it is that? There is nothing worrying you? Nothing on your mind?"

' "On my mind? What should be on my mind?"

'She spoke fiercely and suspiciously.

' "Worry is a cause of sleeplessness sometimes," I said lightly.

'She seemed to brood for a moment.

' "Do you mean worrying over the future, or worrying over the past, which can't be altered?"

' "Either."

' "Only it wouldn't be any good worrying over the past. You couldn't bring back – Oh! what's the use! One mustn't think. One must not think."

'I prescribed her a mild sleeping draught and made my adieu. As I went away I wondered not a little over the words she had spoken. "You couldn't bring back –" What? Or *who*?

'I think that last interview prepared me in a way for what was to come. I didn't expect it, of course, but when it happened, I wasn't surprised. Because, you see, Mary Barton struck me all along as a conscientious woman – not a weak sinner, but a woman with convictions, who would act up to them, and who would not relent as long as she still believed in them. I fancied that in the last conversation we had she was beginning to doubt her own convictions. I know her words suggested to me that she was feeling the first faint beginnings of that terrible soul-searcher – remorse.

'The thing happened in Cornwall, in a small watering-place, rather deserted at that season of the year. It must have been – let me see – late March. I read about it in the papers. A lady had been staying at a small hotel there – a Miss Barton. She had been very odd and peculiar in her manner. That had been noticed by all. At night she would walk up and down her room, muttering to herself, and not allowing the people on either side of her to sleep. She had called on the vicar one day and had told him that she had a communication of the gravest importance to make to him. She had, she said, committed a crime. Then, instead of proceeding, she had stood up abruptly and said she would call another day. The vicar put her down as being slightly mental, and did not take her self-accusation seriously.

'The very next morning she was found to be missing from her room. A note was left addressed to the coroner. It ran as follows: 'I tried to speak to the vicar yesterday, to confess all, but was not allowed. She would not let me. I can make amends only one way – a life for a life; and my life must go the same way as hers did. I, too, must drown in the deep sea. I believed I was justified. I see now that that was not so. If I desire Amy's forgiveness I must go to her. Let no one be blamed for my death – Mary Barton.

'Her clothes were found lying on the beach in a secluded cove nearby, and it seemed clear that she had undressed there and swum resolutely out to sea where the current was known to be dangerous, sweeping one down the coast.

'The body was not recovered, but after a time leave was given to presume death. She was a rich woman, her estate being proved at a hundred thousand pounds. Since she died intestate it all went to her next of kin – a family of cousins in Australia. The papers made discreet references to the tragedy in the Canary Islands, putting forward the theory that the death of Miss Durrant had unhinged her friend's brain. At the inquest the usual verdict of *Suicide whilst temporarily insane* was returned.

'And so the curtain falls on the tragedy of Amy Durrant and Mary Barton.'

There was a long pause and then Jane Helier gave a great gasp.

'Oh, but you mustn't stop there – just at the most interesting part. Go on.'

'But you see, Miss Helier, this isn't a serial story. This is real life; and real life stops just where it chooses.'

'But I don't want it to,' said Jane. 'I want to know.'

'This is where we use our brains, Miss Helier,' explained Sir Henry. 'Why did Mary Barton kill her companion? That's the problem Dr Lloyd has set us.'

'Oh, well,' said Miss Helier, 'she might have killed her for lots of reasons. I mean – oh, I don't know. She might have got on her nerves, or else she got jealous, although Dr Lloyd doesn't mention any men, but still on the boat out – well, you know what everyone says about boats and sea voyages.'

Miss Helier paused, slightly out of breath, and it was borne in upon her audience that the outside of Jane's charming head was distinctly superior to the inside.

'I would like to have a lot of guesses,' said Mrs Bantry. 'But I suppose I must confine myself to one. Well, I think that Miss Barton's father made all his money out of ruining Amy Durrant's father, so Amy determined to have her revenge. Oh, no, that's the wrong way round. How tiresome! Why does the rich employer kill the humble companion? I've got it. Miss Barton had a young brother who shot himself for love of Amy Durrant. Miss Barton waits her time. Amy comes down in the world. Miss B. engages her as companion and takes her to the Canaries and accomplishes her revenge. How's that?'

'Excellent,' said Sir Henry. 'Only we don't know that Miss Barton ever had a young brother.'

'We deduce that,' said Mrs Bantry. 'Unless she had a young brother there's no motive. So she must have had a young brother. Do you see, Watson*?'

'That's all very fine, Dolly,' said her husband. 'But it's only a guess.'

'Of course it is,' said Mrs Bantry. 'That's all we can do – guess. We haven't got any clues. Go on, dear, have a guess yourself.'

'Upon my word, I don't know what to say. But I think there's something in Miss Helier's suggestion that they fell out about a man. Look here, Dolly, it was probably some high church parson. They both embroidered him a cope or something, and he wore the Durrant woman's first. Depend upon it, it was something like that. Look how she went off to a parson at the end. These women all lose their heads over a good-looking clergyman. You hear of it over and over again.'

'I think I must try to make my explanation a little more subtle,' said Sir Henry, 'though I admit it's only a guess. I suggest that Miss Barton was always mentally unhinged. There are more cases like that than you would imagine. Her mania grew stronger and she began to believe it her duty to rid the world of certain persons – possibly what is termed unfortunate females. Nothing much is known about Miss Durrant's past. So very possibly she *had* a past – an "unfortunate" one. Miss Barton learns of this and decides on extermination. Later, the righteousness of her act begins to trouble her and she is overcome by remorse. Her end shows her to be completely unhinged. Now, do say you agree with me, Miss Marple.'

'I'm afraid I don't, Sir Henry,' said Miss Marple, smiling apologetically. 'I think her end shows her to have been a very clever and resourceful woman.'

Jane Helier interrupted with a little scream.

'Oh! I've been so stupid. May I guess again? Of course it must have been that. Blackmail! The companion woman was blackmailing her. Only I don't see why Miss Marple says it was clever of her to kill herself. I can't see that at all.'

'Ah!' said Sir Henry. 'You see, Miss Marple knew a case just like it in St Mary Mead.'

'You always laugh at me, Sir Henry,' said Miss Marple reproachfully. 'I must confess it does remind me, just a little, of old Mrs Trout. She drew the old age pension, you know, for three old women who were dead, in different parishes.'

'It sounds a most complicated and resourceful crime,' said Sir Henry. 'But it doesn't seem to me to throw any light upon our present problem.'

'Of course not,' said Miss Marple. 'It wouldn't – to you. But some of the families were very poor, and the old age pension was a great boon to the children. I know it's difficult for anyone outside to understand. But what I really meant was that the whole thing hinged upon one old woman being so like any other old woman.'

'Eh?' said Sir Henry, mystified.

'I always explain things so badly. What I mean is that when Dr Lloyd described the two ladies first, he didn't know which was which, and I don't suppose anyone else in the hotel did. They would have, of course, after a day or so, but the very next day one of the two was drowned, and if the one who was left said she was Miss Barton, I don't suppose it would ever occur to anyone that she mightn't be.'

'You think – Oh! I see,' said Sir Henry slowly.

'It's the only natural way of thinking of it. Dear Mrs Bantry began that way just now. Why *should* the rich employer kill the humble companion? It's so much more likely to be the other way about. I mean – that's the way things happen.'

'Is it?' said Sir Henry. 'You shock me.'

'But of course,' went on Miss Marple, 'she would have to wear Miss Barton's clothes, and they would probably be a little tight on her, so that her general appearance would look as though she had got a little fatter. That's why I asked that question. A gentleman would be sure to think it was the lady who had got fatter, and not the clothes that had got smaller – though that isn't quite the right way of putting it.'

'But if Amy Durrant killed Miss Barton, what did she gain by it?' asked Mrs Bantry. 'She couldn't keep up the deception for ever.'

'She only kept it up for another month or so,' pointed out Miss Marple. 'And during that time I expect she travelled, keeping away from anyone who might know her. That's what I meant by saying that one lady of a certain age looks so like another. I don't suppose the different photograph on her passport was ever noticed – you know what passports are. And then in March, she went down to this Cornish place and began to act queerly and draw attention to herself so that when people found her clothes on the beach and read her last letter they shouldn't think of the commonsense conclusion.'

'Which was?' asked Sir Henry.

'No *body*,' said Miss Marple firmly. 'That's the thing that would stare you in the face, if there weren't such a lot of red herrings to draw you off the trail – including the suggestion of foul play and remorse. *No body*. That was the real significant fact.'

'Do you mean –' said Mrs Bantry – 'do you mean that there wasn't any remorse? That there wasn't – that she didn't drown herself?'

'Not she!' said Miss Marple. 'It's just Mrs Trout over again. Mrs Trout was very good at red herrings, but she met her match in me. And I can see through your remorse-driven Miss Barton. Drown herself? Went off to Australia, if I'm any good at guessing.'

'You are, Miss Marple,' said Dr Lloyd. 'Undoubtedly you are. Now it again took me quite by surprise. Why, you could have knocked me down with a feather that day in Melbourne.'

'Was that what you spoke of as a final coincidence?'

Dr Lloyd nodded.

'Yes, it was rather rough luck on Miss Barton – or Miss Amy Durrant – whatever you like to call her. I became a ship's doctor for a while, and landing in Melbourne, the first person I saw as I walked down the street was the lady I thought had been drowned in Cornwall. She saw the game was up as far as I was concerned, and she did the bold thing – took me into her confidence. A curious woman, completely lacking, I suppose, in some moral sense. She was the eldest of a family of nine, all wretchedly poor. They had applied once for help to their rich cousin in England and been repulsed, Miss Barton having quarrelled with their father. Money was wanted desperately, for the three youngest children were delicate and wanted expensive medical treatment. Amy Barton then and there seems to have decided on her plan of cold-blooded murder. She set out for England, working her passage over as a children's nurse. She obtained the situation of companion to Miss Barton, calling herself Amy Durrant. She engaged a room and put some furniture into it so as to create more of a personality for herself. The drowning plan was a sudden inspiration. She had been waiting for some opportunity to present itself. Then she staged the final scene of the drama and returned to Australia, and in due time she and her brothers and sisters inherited Miss Barton's money as next of kin.'

'A very bold and perfect crime,' said Sir Henry. 'Almost *the* perfect crime. If it had been Miss Barton who had died in the Canaries, suspicion might attach to Amy Durrant and her connection with the Barton family might have been discovered; but the change of identity and the double crime, as you may call it, effectually did away with that. Yes, almost the perfect crime.'

'What happened to her?' asked Mrs Bantry. 'What did you do in the matter, Dr Lloyd?'

'I was in a very curious position, Mrs Bantry. Of evidence as the law understands it, I still have very little. Also, there were certain signs, plain to me as a medical man, that though strong and vigorous in appearance, the lady was not long for this world. I went home with her and saw the rest of the family – a charming family, devoted to their eldest sister and without an idea in their heads that she might prove to have committed a crime. Why bring sorrow on them when I could prove nothing. The lady's admission to me was unheard by anyone else. I let Nature take its course. Miss Amy Barton died six months after my meeting with her. I have often wondered if she was cheerful and unrepentant up to the last.'

'Surely not,' said Mrs Bantry

'I expect so,' said Miss Marple. 'Mrs Trout was.'

Jane Helier gave herself a little shake.

'Well,' she said. 'It's very, very thrilling. I don't quite understand now who drowned which. And how does this Mrs Trout come into it?'

'She doesn't, my dear,' said Miss Marple. 'She was only a person – not a very nice person – in the village.'

'Oh!' said Jane. 'In the village. But nothing ever happens in a village, does it?' She sighed. 'I'm sure I shouldn't have any brains at all if I lived in a village.'

NOTES

Scotland Yard (p12)

the headquarters of the London police force and the Criminal Investigation Department

Baedeker (p14)

a famous series of travel guides, first published by the German Karl Baedeker in 1827

Bond Street (p14)

a street in London, famous for expensive and fashionable shops

principal boy in the pantomime (p15)

pantomimes usually have a hero played by a girl in tights and a short costume which shows off the legs

Watson (p25)

Dr Watson is the friend of Sherlock Holmes in the Conan Doyle detective stories; Mrs Bantry is trying to think like Sherlock Holmes, and so addresses her husband as though he were Dr Watson

DISCUSSION

1   What wrong conclusions are reached by the other guests as they try to solve the mystery? Which of the guesses do you find the most plausible explanation? Does any guess come near the truth?

2   At what point in the story does Miss Marple apparently guess the answer to the mystery? What question does she ask that shows this? One particular fact she sees as confirmation of her theory. What is it, and why is it significant?

3   The coincidence of Dr Lloyd happening to bump into Amy Durrant later in Australia is certainly very strange. Did you find this coincidence rather unrealistic? Even if it is, does it matter? Can a writer be allowed such devices for the sake of a good story?

LANGUAGE FOCUS

1   Find these expressions in the text of the story and then rephrase them in your own words.

ministered to the ailments of (p11)

racked his brains (p11)
wallow in crime (p11)
a hotbed of crime and vice (p12)
inclined to scragginess (p14)
a tremendous commotion (p16)
next of kin (p24)
you could have knocked me down with a feather (p28)
was not long for this world (p29)

2 People's characters can often be described or suggested by just a few
   simple phrases or remarks. Find these quotations in the story and say
   what they tell you about the characters concerned.

   Colonel Bantry: *he laughed a loud hearty military laugh* (p11)
   Miss Marple: *her eyes twinkled a little* (p11)
   Jane Helier: *she applied some lipstick and waited expectantly* (p12)
   Mrs Bantry: *'It makes me forget how old and fat I am'* (p15)
   Sir Henry: *'I think I must try to make my explanation a little more
   subtle'* (p25)

ACTIVITIES

1 Imagine that you are Dr Lloyd and you have decided that you should
   in fact tell the authorities what really happened, while Amy Durrant
   is still alive. Write a concise report for the police, giving all the facts.

2 Do you think Dr Lloyd was right not to inform the police of Amy
   Durrant's crime, or should she have been punished by the courts?
   Imagine that Amy was in fact arrested for the murder of Miss Mary
   Barton. Depending on your point of view, write some notes for the
   speech either for the defence, or the prosecution, at her trial.

THE CASE FOR THE DEFENCE

THE AUTHOR

Grahame Greene was born in 1904. He worked for various newspapers, was an intelligence agent in the Second World War, and frequently travelled in remote and dangerous places. He wrote novels, short stories, plays, and travel books. Among his lighter novels, which Greene called 'entertainments', are *Stamboul Train*, *A Gun for Sale*, and *The Third Man*, which was made into a famous film. Greene himself preferred his other novels, which reflect his intense interest in religious and moral issues (he was a Roman Catholic convert). These powerful and sombre novels include *Brighton Rock*, *The Power and the Glory*, *The Heart of the Matter*, *A Burnt-out Case*, and *The Human Factor*. Greene died in 1991.

THE STORY

Some crime stories deal not with the murder itself, but with the trial when the murderer is brought to justice – or not, as the case may be. It all depends on the strength of the evidence and the reliability of the witnesses. According to English law, people are innocent until they are proved guilty. It is the defence lawyer's job to challenge the evidence, to shake the witnesses' confidence, to persuade the jury that his client is *not* guilty 'beyond all reasonable doubt'.

The accused in this story will be sentenced to death by hanging if the jury find him guilty. At the beginning it seems an open-and-shut case, according to the journalist telling us the story. Surely no defence lawyer could challenge this evidence, shake these witnesses' certainty . . .

THE CASE FOR THE DEFENCE

It was the strangest murder trial I ever attended. They named it the Peckham* murder in the headlines, though Northwood Street, where the old woman was found battered to death, was not strictly speaking in Peckham. This was not one of those cases of circumstantial evidence in which you feel the jurymen's* anxiety – because mistakes *have* been made – like domes of silence muting the court. No, this murderer was all but found with the body: no one present when the Crown counsel* outlined his case believed that the man in the dock stood any chance at all.

He was a heavy stout man with bulging bloodshot eyes. All his muscles seemed to be in his thighs. Yes, an ugly customer, one you wouldn't forget in a hurry – and that was an important point because the Crown proposed to call four witnesses who hadn't forgotten him, who had seen him hurrying away from the little red villa in Northwood Street. The clock had just struck two in the morning.

Mrs Salmon in 15 Northwood Street had been unable to sleep: she heard a door click shut and thought it was her own gate. So she went to the window and saw Adams (that was his name) on the steps of Mrs Parker's house. He had just come out and he was wearing gloves. He had a hammer in his hand and she saw him drop it into the laurel bushes by the front gate. But before he moved away, he had looked up – at her window. The fatal instinct that tells a man when he is watched exposed him in the light of a street-lamp to her gaze – his eyes suffused with horrifying and brutal fear, like an animal's when you raise a whip. I talked afterwards to Mrs Salmon, who naturally after the astonishing verdict went in fear herself. As I imagine did all the witnesses – Henry MacDougall, who had been driving home from Benfleet late and nearly ran Adams down at the corner of Northwood Street. Adams was walking in the middle of the road looking dazed. And old Mr Wheeler, who lived next door to Mrs Parker, at No. 12, and was wakened by a noise – like a chair falling – through the thin-as-paper villa wall, and got up and looked out of the window, just as Mrs Salmon had done, saw Adams's back and, as he turned, those bulging eyes. In Laurel Avenue he had been seen by yet another witness – his luck was badly out; he might as well have committed the crime in broad daylight.

'I understand,' counsel said, 'that the defence proposes to plead mistaken identity. Adams's wife will tell you that he was with her at two in the morning on February 14, but after you have heard the witnesses for the Crown and examined carefully the features of the prisoner, I do not think you will be prepared to admit the possibility of a mistake.'

It was all over, you would have said, but the hanging.

After the formal evidence had been given by the policeman who had found the body and the surgeon who examined it, Mrs Salmon was called. She was the ideal witness, with her slight Scotch accent and her expression of honesty, care and kindness.

The counsel for the Crown brought the story gently out. She spoke very firmly. There was no malice in her, and no sense of importance at standing there in the Central Criminal Court with a judge in scarlet hanging on her words and the reporters writing them down. Yes, she said, and then she had gone downstairs and rung up the police station.

'And do you see the man here in court?'

She looked straight at the big man in the dock, who stared hard at her with his pekingese* eyes without emotion.

'Yes,' she said, 'there he is.'

'You are quite certain?'

She said simply, 'I couldn't be mistaken, sir.'

It was all as easy as that.

'Thank you, Mrs Salmon.'

Counsel for the defence rose to cross-examine. If you had reported as many murder trials as I have, you would have known beforehand what line he would take. And I was right, up to a point.

'Now, Mrs Salmon, you must remember that a man's life may depend on your evidence.'

'I do remember it, sir.'

'Is your eyesight good?'

'I have never had to wear spectacles, sir.'

'You are a woman of fifty-five?'

'Fifty-six, sir.'

'And the man you saw was on the other side of the road?'

'Yes, sir.'

'And it was two o'clock in the morning. You must have remarkable eyes, Mrs Salmon?'

'No, sir. There was moonlight, and when the man looked up, he had the lamplight on his face.'

'And you have no doubt whatever that the man you saw is the prisoner?'

I couldn't make out what he was at. He couldn't have expected any other answer than the one he got.

'None whatever, sir. It isn't a face one forgets.'

Counsel took a look round the court for a moment. Then he said, 'Do you mind, Mrs Salmon, examining again the people in court? No, not the prisoner. Stand up, please, Mr Adams,' and there at the back of the court with thick stout body and muscular legs and a pair of bulging eyes, was the exact image of the man in the dock. He was even dressed the same – tight blue suit and striped tie.

'Now think very carefully, Mrs Salmon. Can you still swear that the man you saw drop the hammer in Mrs Parker's garden was the prisoner – and not this man, who is his twin brother?'

Of course she couldn't. She looked from one to the other and didn't say a word.

There the big brute sat in the dock with his legs crossed, and there he stood too at the back of the court and they both stared at Mrs Salmon. She shook her head.

What we saw then was the end of the case. There wasn't a witness prepared to swear that it was the prisoner he'd seen. And the brother? He had his alibi, too; he was with his wife.

And so the man was acquitted for lack of evidence. But whether – if he did the murder and not his brother – he was punished or not, I don't know. That extraordinary day had an extraordinary end. I followed Mrs Salmon out of court and we got wedged in the crowd who were waiting, of course, for the twins. The police tried to drive the crowd away, but all they could do was keep the road-way clear for traffic. I learned later that they tried to get the twins to leave by a back way, but they wouldn't. One of them – no one knew which – said, 'I've been acquitted, haven't I?' and they walked bang out of the front entrance. Then it happened. I don't know how, though I was only six feet away. The crowd moved and somehow one of the twins got pushed on to the road right in front of a bus.

He gave a squeal like a rabbit and that was all; he was dead, his skull smashed just as Mrs Parker's had been. Divine vengeance? I wish I knew. There was the other Adams getting on his feet from beside the body and looking straight over at Mrs Salmon. He was crying, but whether he was the murderer or the innocent man nobody will ever be able to tell. But if you were Mrs Salmon, could you sleep at night?

NOTES

Peckham (p35)
  a district in London
jurymen (p35)
  a group of people (nowadays both men and women) in a court of justice,
  who must listen to the evidence and decide if the accused is innocent or
  guilty
Crown counsel (p35)
  a barrister (lawyer) appointed by the government to conduct the case
  for the prosecution
pekingese (p36)
  a type of small dog with large bulging eyes

DISCUSSION

1   Do you think Adams's acquittal was right, legally or morally?

2   What would you do if you were Mrs Salmon, after the trial and the
    death of one of the Adams brothers?

3   Do you think that the man who died was deliberately pushed in front
    of the bus? And if so, who do you think pushed him? Was it a
    bystander, the guilty brother, or the innocent brother? What might
    their motives be?

LANGUAGE FOCUS

1   Look through the story and find all the words associated with
    lawcourts and justice (e.g. *trial, case, circumstantial evidence, court,
    dock, witness, verdict,* and so on). Can any of these words have other
    meanings, or be used in contexts not associated with the law?

2   Find these expressions in the story and then rephrase them in your
    own words.

      an ugly customer (p35)
      his luck was badly out (p36)
      hanging on her words (p36)
      I couldn't make out what he was at (p37)
      they walked bang out of the front entrance (p38)

ACTIVITIES

1　The case for the defence rests only on the fact that *both* brothers can't have committed the crime; it is not disputed that *one* of them did the murder. Imagine that the accident with the bus did not happen and that the two brothers walk away alive. The next day the police arrest both of them and charge both with the murder.

　　Now write a new ending for the story. How do the police try to break the brothers' alibis, and get one to confess, or one to accuse the other? Do they interrogate them separately, put them together in a prison cell and eavesdrop on their conversations, look for fresh evidence? Do the police win, or the Adams brothers?

2　This story was written while capital punishment (execution by the state) was still law in Britain. Capital punishment for murder was abolished in 1965, but the question is still discussed from time to time by Parliament.

　　It is a difficult question – difficult in every sense. For the moment, try to forget your personal opinion, and write down three arguments for capital punishment, and three arguments against.

A Glowing Future

The Author

Ruth Rendell was born in 1930, and worked for some time
as a journalist. Her traditional detective novels include
From Doon with Death, *The Speaker of Mandarin*, *Wolf
to the Slaughter*. These feature Detective Chief Inspector
Wexford, a steady, unshockable policeman, who solves
crimes in an imaginary Sussex village; the television series
of Inspector Wexford mysteries is extremely popular. She
also writes chilling psychological thrillers, grim stories of
obsession and paranoia, such as *A Judgement in Stone* and
Talking to Strange Men. Among her collections of short
stories are *The Fever Tree*, *The Fallen Curtain*, and *The
New Girlfriend*. She has won several awards for her work,
and her books have been translated into many languages.

The Story

Some murders are planned beforehand, in cold blood, and
there is usually little sympathy for that kind of murderer.
But some murders are not planned; they happen on the spur
of the moment, in the heat and rage and despair of some
terrible passion. Sometimes the victim has provoked that
passion, and a plea of provocation is entered in the
murderer's defence.

Maurice has a wonderful future in front of him – a
three-month tour of Europe, seeing the sights and the girls,
then back to Australia to a job, marriage, and a responsible
family life. There is just one thing he has to do before he
sets off from London – collect his belongings from the flat
he used to share with Betsy . . .

A GLOWING FUTURE

'Six should be enough,' he said. 'We'll say six tea chests, then, and one trunk. If you'll deliver them tomorrow, I'll get the stuff all packed and maybe your people could pick them up Wednesday.' He made a note on a bit of paper. 'Fine,' he said. 'Round about lunchtime tomorrow.'

She hadn't moved. She was still sitting in the big oak-armed chair at the far end of the room. He made himself look at her and he managed a kind of grin, pretending all was well.

'No trouble,' he said. 'They're very efficient.'

'I couldn't believe,' she said, 'that you'd really do it. Not until I heard you on the phone. I wouldn't have thought it possible. You'll really pack up all those things and have them sent off to her.'

They were going to have to go over it all again. Of course they were. It wouldn't stop until he'd got the things out and himself out, away from London and her for good. And he wasn't going to argue or make long defensive speeches. He lit a cigarette and waited for her to begin, thinking that the pubs would be opening in an hour's time and he could go out then and get a drink.

'I don't understand why you came here at all,' she said.

He didn't answer. He was still holding the cigarette box, and now he closed its lid, feeling the coolness of the onyx on his fingertips.

She had gone white. 'Just to get your things? Maurice, did you come back just for that?'

'They are my things,' he said evenly.

'You could have sent someone else. Even if you'd written to me and asked me to do it –'

'I never write letters,' he said.

She moved then. She made a little fluttering with her hand in front of her mouth. 'As if I didn't know!' She gasped, and making a great effort she steadied her voice. 'You were in Australia for a year, a whole year, and you never wrote to me once.'

'I phoned.'

'Yes, twice. The first time to say you loved me and missed me and were longing to come back to me and would I wait for you and there wasn't anyone else was there? And the second time, a week ago, to say you'd be here by Saturday and could I – could I put you up. My God, I'd lived with you for two years, we were practically married, and then you phone and ask if I could put you up!'

'Words,' he said. 'How would you have put it?'

'For one thing, I'd have mentioned Patricia. Oh, yes, I'd have mentioned her. I'd have had the decency, the common humanity, for that. D'you know what I thought when you said you were coming? I ought to know by now how peculiar he is, I thought, how detached, not writing or phoning or anything. But that's Maurice, that's the man I love, and he's coming back to me and we'll get married and I'm so happy!'

'I did tell you about Patricia.'

'Not until after you'd made love to me first.'

He winced. It had been a mistake, that. Of course he hadn't meant to touch her beyond the requisite greeting kiss. But she was very attractive and he was used to her and she seemed to expect it – and oh, what the hell. Women never could understand about men and sex. And there was only one bed, wasn't there? A hell of a scene there'd have been that first night if he'd suggested sleeping on the sofa in here.

'You made love to me,' she said. 'You were so passionate, it was just like it used to be, and then the next morning you told me. You'd got a resident's permit to stay in Australia, you'd got a job all fixed up, you'd met a girl you wanted to marry. Just like that you told me, over breakfast. Have you ever been smashed in the face, Maurice? Have you ever had your dreams trodden on?'

'Would you rather I'd waited longer? As for being smashed in the face –' he rubbed his cheekbone '– that's quite a punch you pack.'

She shuddered. She got up and began slowly and stiffly to pace the room. 'I hardly touched you. I wish I'd killed you!' By a small table she stopped. There was a china figurine on it, a bronze paperknife, an onyx pen jar that matched the ashtray. 'All those things,' she said. 'I looked after them for you. I treasured them. And now you're going to have them all shipped out to her. The things we lived with. I used to look at them and think, Maurice bought that when we went to – oh God, I can't believe it. Sent to her!'

He nodded, staring at her. 'You can keep the big stuff,' he said. 'You're specially welcome to the sofa. I've tried sleeping on it for two nights and I never want to see the bloody thing again.'

She picked up the china figurine and hurled it at him. It didn't hit him because he ducked and let it smash against the wall, just missing a framed drawing. 'Mind the Lowry*,' he said laconically, 'I paid a lot of money for that.'

She flung herself onto the sofa and burst into sobs. She thrashed about, hammering the cushions with her fists. He wasn't going to be moved by that – he wasn't going to be moved at all. Once he'd packed those things, he'd be off to spend the next three months touring Europe. A free man, free for the sights and the fun and the girls, for a last fling of wild oats*. After that, back to Patricia and a home and a job and responsibility. It was a glowing future which this hysterical woman wasn't going to mess up.

'Shut up, Betsy, for God's sake,' he said. He shook her roughly by the shoulder, and then he went out because it was now eleven and he could get a drink.

Betsy made herself some coffee and washed her swollen eyes. She walked about, looking at the ornaments and the books, the glasses and vases and lamps, which he would take from her tomorrow. It wasn't that she much minded losing them, the things themselves, but the barrenness which would be left, and the knowing that they would all be Patricia's.

In the night she had got up, found his wallet, taken out the photographs of Patricia, and torn them up. But she remembered the face, pretty and hard and greedy, and she thought of those bright eyes widening as Patricia unpacked the tea chests, the predatory hands scrabbling for more treasures in the trunk. Doing it all perhaps before Maurice himself got there, arranging the lamps and the glasses and the ornaments in their home for his delight when at last he came.

He would marry her, of course. I suppose she thinks he's faithful to her, Betsy thought, the way I once thought he was faithful to me. I know better now. Poor stupid fool, she doesn't know what he did the first moment he was alone with her, or what he would do in France and Italy. That would be a nice wedding present to give her, wouldn't it, along with all the pretty bric-a-brac in the trunk?

Well, why not? Why not rock their marriage before it had even begun? A letter. A letter to be concealed in, say, that blue-and-white ginger jar. She sat down to write. Dear Patricia – what a stupid way to begin, the way you had to begin a letter even to your enemy.

Dear Patricia: I don't know what Maurice has told you about me, but we have been living here as lovers ever since he arrived. To be more explicit, I mean we have made love, have slept together. Maurice is incapable of being faithful to anyone. If you don't believe me, ask yourself why, if he didn't want me, he didn't stay in a hotel. That's all. Yours – and she signed her name and felt a little better, well enough and steady enough to take a bath and get herself some lunch.

Six tea chests and a trunk arrived on the following day. The chests smelled of tea and had drifts of tea leaves lying in the bottom of them. The trunk was made of silver-coloured metal and had clasps of gold-coloured metal. It was rather a beautiful object, five feet long, three feet high, two feet wide, and the lid fitted so securely it seemed a hermetic sealing.

Maurice began to pack at two o'clock. He used tissue paper and newspapers. He filled the tea chests with kitchen equipment and cups and plates and cutlery, with books, with those clothes of his he had left behind him a year before. Studiously, and with a certain grim pleasure, he avoided everything Betsy might have insisted was hers – the poor cheap things, the stainless steel spoons and forks, the Woolworth pottery, the awful coloured sheets, red and orange and olive, that he had always loathed. He and Patricia would sleep in white linen.

Betsy didn't help him. She watched, chain-smoking. He nailed the lids on the chests and on each lid he wrote in white paint his address in Australia. But he didn't paint in the letters of his own name. He painted Patricia's. This wasn't done to needle Betsy but he was glad to see it was needling her.

He hadn't come back to the flat till one that morning, and of course he didn't have a key. Betsy had refused to let him in, had left him down there in the street, and he had to sit in the car he'd hired till seven. She looked as if she hadn't slept either. Miss Patricia Gordon, he wrote, painting fast and skilfully.

'Don't forget your ginger jar,' said Betsy. 'I don't want it.'

'That's for the trunk.' Miss Patricia Gordon, 23 Burwood Park Avenue, Kew, Victoria, Australia 3101. 'All the pretty things are going in the trunk. I intend it as a special present for Patricia.'

The Lowry came down and was carefully padded and wrapped.

He wrapped the onyx ashtray and the pen jar, the alabaster bowl, the bronze paperknife, the tiny Chinese cups, the tall hock glasses. The china figurine, alas . . . he opened the lid of the trunk.

'I hope the customs open it!' Betsy shouted at him. 'I hope they confiscate things and break things! I'll pray every night for it to go to the bottom of the sea before it gets there!'

'The sea,' he said, 'is a risk I must take. As for the customs – ' He smiled. 'Patricia works for them, she's a customs officer – didn't I tell you? I very much doubt if they'll even glance inside.' He wrote a label and pasted it on the side of the trunk. Miss Patricia Gordon, 23 Burwood Park Avenue, Kew . . . 'And now I'll have to go out and get a padlock. Keys, please. If you try to keep me out this time, I'll call the police. I'm still the legal tenant of this flat remember.'

She gave him the keys. When he had gone she put her letter in the ginger jar. She hoped he would close the trunk at once, but he didn't. He left it open, the lid thrown back, the new padlock dangling from the gold-coloured clasp.

'Is there anything to eat?' he said.

'Go and find your own bloody food! Go and find some other woman to feed you!'

He liked her to be angry and fierce; it was her love he feared. He came back at midnight to find the flat in darkness, and he lay down on the sofa with the tea chests standing about him like defences, like barricades, the white paint showing faintly in the dark. Miss Patricia Gordon . . .

Presently Betsy came in. She didn't put on the light. She wound her way between the chests, carrying a candle in a saucer which she set down on the trunk. In the candlelight, wearing a long white nightgown, she looked like a ghost, like some wandering madwoman, a Mrs Rochester*, a Woman in White*.

'Maurice.'

'Go away, Betsy, I'm tired.'

'Maurice, please. I'm sorry I said all those things. I'm sorry I locked you out.'

'OK, I'm sorry too. It's a mess, and maybe I shouldn't have done it the way I did. But the best way is for me just to go and my things to go and make a clean split. Right? And now will you please be a good girl and go away and let me get some sleep?'

What happened next he hadn't bargained for. It hadn't crossed his mind. Men don't understand about women and sex. She threw herself on him, clumsily, hungrily. She pulled his shirt open and began kissing his neck and his chest, holding his head, crushing her mouth to his mouth, lying on top of him and gripping his legs with her knees.

He gave her a savage push. He kicked her away, and she fell and struck her head on the side of the trunk. The candle fell off, flared and died in a pool of wax. In the darkness he cursed floridly. He put on the light and she got up, holding her head where there was a little blood.

'Oh, get out, for God's sake,' he said, and he manhandled her out, slamming the door after her.

In the morning, when she came into the room, a blue bruise on her forehead, he was asleep, fully clothed, spread-eagled on his back. She shuddered at the sight of him. She began to get breakfast but she couldn't eat anything. The coffee made her gag and a great nauseous shiver went through her. When she went back to him he was sitting up on the sofa, looking at his plane ticket to Paris.

'The men are coming for the stuff at ten,' he said as if nothing had happened, 'and they'd better not be late. I have to be at the airport at noon.'

She shrugged. She had been to the depths and she thought he couldn't hurt her any more.

'You'd better close the trunk,' she said absent-mindedly.

'All in good time.' His eyes gleamed. 'I've got a letter to put in yet.'

Her head bowed, the place where it was bruised sore and swollen, she looked loweringly at him. 'You never write letters.'

'Just a note. One can't send a present without a note to accompany it, can one?'

He pulled the ginger jar out of the trunk, screwed up her letter without even glancing at it, and threw it on the floor. Rapidly yet ostentatiously and making sure that Betsy could see, he scrawled across a sheet of paper: *All this is for you, darling Patricia, for ever and ever.*

'How I hate you,' she said.

'You could have fooled me.' He took a large angle lamp out of the trunk and set it on the floor. He slipped the note into the ginger jar, rewrapped it, tucked the jar in between the towels and cushions which padded the fragile objects. 'Hatred isn't the word I'd use to describe the way you came after me last night.'

She made no answer. Perhaps he should have put a heavy object like that lamp in one of the chests, perhaps he should open up one of the chests now. He turned round for the lamp. It wasn't there. She was holding it in both hands.

'I want that, please.'

'Have you ever been smashed in the face, Maurice?' she said breathlessly, and she raised the lamp and struck him with it full on the forehead. He staggered and she struck him again, and again and again, raining blows on his face and his head. He screamed. He sagged, covering his face with bloody hands. Then with all her strength she gave him a great swinging blow and he fell to his knees, rolled over and at last was stilled and silenced.

There was quite a lot of blood, though it quickly stopped flowing. She stood there looking at him and she was sobbing. Had

she been sobbing all the time? She was covered with blood. She
tore off her clothes and dropped them in a heap around her. For
a moment she knelt beside him, naked and weeping, rocking
backwards and forwards, speaking his name, biting her fingers
that were sticky with his blood.

But self-preservation is the primal instinct, more powerful than
love or sorrow, hatred or regret. The time was nine o'clock, and in
an hour those men would come. Betsy fetched water in a bucket,
detergent, cloths and a sponge. The hard work, the great
cleansing, stopped her tears, quieted her heart and dulled her
thoughts. She thought of nothing, working frenziedly, her mind a
blank.

When bucket after bucket of reddish water had been poured
down the sink and the carpet was soaked but clean, the lamp
washed and dried and polished, she threw her clothes into the
basket in the bathroom and had a bath. She dressed carefully and
brushed her hair. Eight minutes to ten. Everything was clean and
she had opened the window, but the dead thing still lay there on
a pile of reddened newspapers.

'I loved him,' she said aloud, and she clenched her fists. 'I hated
him.'

The men were punctual. They came at ten sharp. They carried
the six tea chests and the silver-coloured trunk with the
gold-coloured clasps downstairs.

When they had gone and their van had driven away, Betsy sat
down on the sofa. She looked at the angle lamp, the onyx pen jar
and ashtray, the ginger jar, the alabaster bowls, the hock glasses,
the bronze paperknife, the little Chinese cups, and the Lowry that
was back on the wall. She was quite calm now and she didn't
really need the brandy she had poured for herself.

Of the past she thought not at all and the present seemed to
exist only as a palpable nothingness, a thick silence that lay

around her. She thought of the future, of three months hence, and into the silence she let forth a steady, rather toneless peal of laughter. Miss Patricia Gordon, 23 Burwood Park Avenue, Kew, Victoria, Australia 3101. The pretty, greedy, hard face, the hands so eager to undo that padlock and prise open those golden clasps to find the treasure within . . .

And how interesting that treasure would be in three months' time, like nothing Miss Patricia Gordon had seen in all her life! It was as well, so that she would recognize it, that it carried on top of it a note in a familiar hand: *All this is for you, darling Patricia, for ever and ever.*

NOTES

Lowry (p45)
L.S. Lowry (1887–1976), a British artist, whose paintings of industrial landscapes now fetch high prices

a last fling of wild oats (p45)
a final period of irresponsible pleasure-seeking (especially in casual love affairs)

Mrs Rochester (p48)
the mad wife of Mr Rochester, the hero of Charlotte Brontë's famous novel, *Jane Eyre*

Woman in White (p48)
a character, supposedly a lunatic, in the novel of that name by Wilkie Collins

DISCUSSION

1 Why do you think Maurice is more attracted to Patricia than to Betsy? Do you think his only reason for returning to London was to collect his possessions?

2 Betsy's emotions and reactions to Maurice's behaviour become more and more uncontrollable as the story progresses. Make a list of the sequence of actions and remarks by Maurice that finally drive her over the edge.

3 What do you think Betsy will do after the end of the story? In three months' time a murder investigation will begin and all the evidence will point to her. Will the 'primal instinct of self-preservation' make her try to hide or run away, or will she just sit and wait, obsessed by the picture of her revenge on Patricia?

4 Do you feel sympathy for either of the two main characters in this story? If so, which one, and why?

LANGUAGE FOCUS

1 Find these expressions in the text of the story and then rephrase them in your own words.

away (from London and her) for good (p43)

could I put you up (p44)
that's quite a punch you pack (p45)
rock their marriage (p46)
chain-smoking (p47)
make a clean split (p49)
It hadn't crossed his mind (p49)
She had been to the depths (p49)
raining blows on his face (p50)

2   The strong emotions in this story are often not described directly, but
    are suggested by the descriptions of physical activity. Find some of the
    words that describe sudden or violent actions, and say what emotions
    you think are suggested. For example:

    Have you ever been smashed in the face?
    She flung herself onto the sofa
    crushing her mouth to his mouth
    slamming the door

ACTIVITIES

1   The viewpoint in the story swings from Maurice to Betsy and back
    again, showing the great lack of understanding or sympathy between
    them. Write a short description of each character, as seen from the
    other's point of view.

2   Imagine you are Betsy's older brother or sister. Betsy phones you on
    Maurice's last evening, when he has packed all his things and gone
    out to get a meal. She tells you everything Maurice has said and done,
    and after the phone call you write her a letter of advice, suggesting
    the best way for her to deal with the situation.

3   When Maurice pushes Betsy away in the middle of the night, imagine
    that she hits her head hard and is killed outright. Maurice is still
    determined not to let her spoil his future. Rewrite the end of the story.

RICOCHET

THE AUTHOR

Angela Noel was born in 1931, and now lives in Lancashire, where she runs a livery stables. Most of her writing consists of short stories for women's magazines in several countries, and she has also published four romantic novels, all set in the English countryside. Her most recent title is *Remember Me*. Her story *Ricochet* was first published in March 1980 in *London Mystery Selection*. Although the story is set in Wales, the idea for it was originally drawn from a newspaper report about a real-life incident concerning two brothers in Spain, one of whom was accused of murdering the other.

THE STORY

Possessiveness seems to be a fundamental characteristic of human beings: the urge to possess things – and people. And if our possessions are taken away from us, our feelings of resentment at life's injustice can be very strong indeed. It is said that there is a potential murderer in all of us, that if the pressures are great enough, anybody can be driven to the ultimate act of violence. It is not a comfortable thought.

In a beautiful Welsh valley Owen Parry has brooded on life's injustice for many years. His resentment is focused on his brother Huw. It is Huw who is married to Rhiannon, Huw who lives in the comfortable farmhouse, Huw who has caused the slaughter of all their sheep. Only Huw stands between Owen and happiness, the possession of all the things that are rightfully his ...

RICOCHET

Owen had planned to wear gloves. He had an ancient pair in brown leather, which he wore for Sunday chapel* in winter. But his farmer's hands were clumsy in them and this was delicate work.

Owen Parry stopped and looked about him with a little rat-smile. Why bother with gloves at all? This was his own cottage, wasn't it? The police would expect to find his fingerprints all over it. These were his two wooden chairs, now standing back to back and apart by a carefully measured distance.

The shot gun was his, too. Of course it bore his fingerprints. Now the gun lay across the backs of the two chairs, firmly held with rope and wire. It pointed at his only door.

The gun was cocked. From the trigger, a string was looped to the door handle. When that door was thrown back, the string would jerk tight. And when did his brother Huw not throw doors wide?

For a moment Owen's stomach welled in him but he held himself taut. Switch on an inviting light, he told himself, and leave the cottage by a window.

His brother would be here before evening chapel.

'To talk about re-stocking the farm,' Owen had lied nervously while persuading him to come.

'Huh, re-stocking, is it?' Huw had grunted. 'Looking ahead, aren't we?'

Both their faces were still grey from the nightmare of foot-and-mouth disease* that had devastated their farm. By compulsory order, their whole flock had been slaughtered. Their dogs too had to go, their beautiful faithful intelligent dogs. Even Beth, whom they all loved best.

Owen sighed at the thought of Beth but her memory

strengthened his will. He had suffered enough. He set off for the
village to create his alibi.

Even now, surrounded by the tragedy of empty hills, he felt his
passion surge for this place he'd always known, for the lovely
sweep of valley, for the curl of polished-steel river, for the
farmhouse with its close family of buildings.

Soon it would all be his and his alone. He would work and care
and live again. The hills would sing with the bleat of a healthy
flock and there would be dogs once more, streaming them down
to the river meadow.

Though there'd never be another bitch quite like Beth. Even
today, heading for the village, Owen imagined he still heard her
barking, barking up at the deserted sheepfold on the hill behind
his cottage.

Some partnership it had been with his brother! It wasn't enough
that Huw had married Rhiannon, the girl they both loved, the
pretty, sympathetic, pliable Rhiannon. Or that Huw and his wife
took over the good stone farmhouse, leaving Owen to move out
to the musty riverside cottage.

Worst of all, after the first year or two, Huw was not even
making Rhiannon happy and their marriage, unblessed by
children, had begun slowly to wither at the edges.

Huw was a blackhaired giant, bass-voiced, rock-strong. To
him, being without child was traumatic, demeaning. He imagined
the village sniggered behind its net curtains. 'There goes Huw
Parry, owns half the valley with his brother, married these five
years and can't get his wife pregnant.'

And who in that lonely valley could the sad Rhiannon turn to
but her brother-in-law? Didn't she know, as any woman knows,
that he'd always loved her?

'Like the river you are, Owen Parry,' she told him, 'slow and
deep.'

As children, both boys had played and danced and kissed with her. But they were children no longer. One day Owen took his sister-in-law in his arms and the dream he had nurtured for all those silent years woke to reality.

But the birth of Margo wrought a change in Huw that stunned both Owen and Rhiannon. Overnight, it seemed, Huw stood tall again. He sang at his work and displayed a tenderness the other two had not known he possessed.

For the second time in his life, Owen had seen Rhiannon slipping from him to cleave to Huw. The old fire smouldered anew, silent and menacing inside him. One day it must blaze.

The slaughter of the flock it was that finally set the fire alight.

None of it need have happened, hadn't Owen said so again and again? One slobbering ewe they'd found, just one, and that they could easily have disposed of in secret. Then with gallons of disinfectant they could have tried, at least they could have tried, to protect the rest of the flock from the scourge of foot-and-mouth.

But oh no! Huw, upright Godfearing chapel man that he was, Huw must call the authorities. Younger and bigger, he'd tossed Owen aside and marched for the telephone. The nightmare had been set in motion. The inspectors came and passed the death sentence on sheep and dogs alike.

'I hope you're satisfied, Huw Parry,' said Owen that night and he felt a lifetime's resentment of his brother slip over the edge into something deeper and much harder to control.

Owen had made one last appeal to Rhiannon. Huw was outside, staring morosely at the river. Margo they could hear in the yard, calling tearfully for the vanished Beth.

'Huw can't bring himself to tell her about having to shoot Beth,' Rhiannon said tenderly, watching her husband from her kitchen window. 'I'll never forget how he looked as he led Beth away and she went, waving that plume tail of hers, obedient to the last. Beth was always Margo's favourite and it broke his heart to have to do it.'

Owen's arm tightened across Rhiannon's shoulders. 'We can't go on like this, love,' he said. 'You've got to tell Huw the truth. Let him find some other farm. We'll re-stock as soon as they'll let us and we'll set up house here like the family we really are.'

He glanced covetously at the firm dry walls, the roominess and solidity of the place, so different from his miserable cottage.

But when his gaze returned to Rhiannon, her blank look killed his hope.

'Is it mad you are, Owen Parry?' she said. 'Would I tell my man to go, after all he's suffered, after all this destruction and grief? Would I rob him of his land and his child –?'

'Whose child?' said Owen.

Rhiannon paled. 'God forgive me, he's as good as a father to her.'

Owen spread his hands. 'It's childless you'd be to this day if you hadn't turned to me.'

She shook her head of long dark hair. 'Oh I know you were good to me when my marriage was going badly, Owen. I needed you then. But Huw and me, we're so much happier now. You must see that. He's a different man. He worships Margo – and I won't let you take her from him. I'll deny every word you say and it's me he'll believe.'

Owen grasped her shoulders, thin under his demanding hands, and shook her. Her dark hair flopped forward, then she threw up her head and defied him.

He wanted to roar at her, 'You have used me like a prize ram!' But he quelled the words. If once he turned Rhiannon against himself, his life would be without meaning.

He'd walked away, sickened by the knowledge of what he must do.

That night Owen wept, alone in his musty cottage, and his deepest distress was for Margo, his brown-eyed elf. No choir ever sang like that child laughing . . .

While Huw lived, Rhiannon would be his wife, Margo his daughter. What choice had they left him? A man could only take – or lose – so much.

Owen brooded for a week, a scheme simmering in his mind.

He might have pulled the trigger himself – but he knew his courage would fail him. Huw had only to look at him with those blazing black eyes of his and Owen would feel his strength of purpose drain away into the ground. And how to convince people it was an accident? No, Huw must be the one to pull the trigger. And hadn't the slaughter of an entire flock, a lifetime's work, been known to drive a man to suicide? Hadn't Huw been morose of late, since their loss? What better place to choose than his brother's home to spare his wife and child from finding his body?

Thus was born the idea of the trap.

Grudgingly, Huw had agreed to come down to Owen's cottage this Sunday afternoon to talk about the farm. Huw would fling open the door and it would all be over. He wouldn't even suffer or know a moment's suspicion. A small price to pay for another's happiness, Owen thought.

Owen would walk back from the village after chapel, clutching his watertight alibi. It would take only minutes to falsify the evidence, to remove all signs of wire and string, and to place the gun in the dead man's hands. Then Owen would run in innocent horror to telephone the police. The widow would weep in his arms.

Now Owen's heart thundered in his breast as he left his cottage and his gun, waiting, behind him.

The village lay freezing in the Sunday afternoon quiet. Though not, apparently, too cold for Mrs Price, Groceries, forever at her door.

'Terrible to be idle, isn't it?' she said, with relish.

Owen stopped. What better witness to his whereabouts this Sunday afternoon, she with her mind like the hoard of a squirrel, packed tight with seeds of suspicion and sweet nuts of scandal?

When at last Mrs Price ran out of chatter, he called on Ma Hughes and asked politely about her arthritis. Ma Hughes offered him tea.

Owen left Ma Hughes when he'd barely enough time to reach chapel. He entered that hushed place, let the door fall to with a thud and broke into a fit of coughing.

Afterwards, his irreverence apparently forgiven, they asked him where Huw was. 'Can't remember when last Huw Parry missed chapel,' they all said.

Owen shook his head and murmured about depression.

Despite the cold, Owen was sweating as he left the lane and slowly crunched back over the crystal grass to his cottage.

He reached his door, put out his hand . . .

No, wait. The gun might still be cocked, if for any reason Huw had failed to come down. Even in death, he didn't trust his brother. He peered nervously in through his lighted window.

Owen's scream split the night.

He burst into the cottage, jaw slack, eyes protruding, hands dragging at his hair. He gaped down at the two sprawled and bloody bodies on his floor.

Margo and the sheepdog Beth.

He prodded the bitch with his shoe and it was rigid. He couldn't touch the child. His own daughter. He covered his face.

His mind was a vortex of horror and bewilderment. Then the truth flashed against his closed lids.

Huw had cheated. He had never slaughtered the bitch as ordered. He must have hidden her. Suddenly Owen recalled that ghostly barking from the sheepfold. Of course! Then today she must have escaped, perhaps found and released by a delighted Margo, and they'd come bounding down the hillside to tell her Uncle Owen the good news . . .

It took only a few minutes to discard the wire and string, reload the gun and blow out the side of his head.

The explosion awoke the sleeping child. Margo started up, crying, as the noise renewed her terror. She looked only at Beth, who had not moved. She remembered trying to keep up with Beth and how the bitch bounded at the cottage door ahead of her, the unbearable noise and how the bitch fell whimpering and twitching. She had flung herself down, fondling Beth, trying to rouse her, getting covered in the animal's blood. She must have cried herself to sleep on the floor.

Now she turned and fled screaming from the cottage. Halfway home, stumbling through the moonlight, she cannoned into Huw.

'Oh Margo, my Margo, I've been searching for you this past two hours!' Huw scooped up the child and carried her joyously home, thanking the Lord for the safety of his beloved daughter.

He decided it was too late now to go and see Owen.

NOTES

chapel (p57)

a building used for Christian worship by members of one of the Nonconformist sects of the Protestant religion (e.g. the Methodists, who are very strong in Wales)

foot-and-mouth disease (p57)

a very infectious disease that affects farm animals; in Britain (though not in other countries) the disease is controlled by the obligatory slaughter of infected animals

DISCUSSION

1 Which do you think was more important for Owen, sole possession and management of the farm, or living with Rhiannon and being able to claim Margo as his own daughter?

2 Why do you think Rhiannon chose to marry Huw rather than Owen? Describe both brothers from her point of view. What is your opinion of her own character? Is she partly to blame for the tragedy? Why, or why not?

3 Do you think that tragedy would have been prevented if Rhiannon and Margo had left Huw and moved in with Owen? What do you think Huw would have done, that 'upright Godfearing chapel man'?

LANGUAGE FOCUS

1 Find the images which are used in the story to describe people in relation to these animals or natural features:

   a rat, rock, a river, fire, a squirrel

   What adjectives can you think of that would create the same effect as these images? Can you think of other animals or natural features which are often used to suggest human characteristics? For example, what do you associate with these things: a storm, a deep pool, a snake, a horse, a lion, a cat?

2 These expressions use a word order that is often used by Welsh people but not by people in other regions. Rephrase them in the usual word order.

- *Like the river you are.*
- *The slaughter of the flock it was that finally set the fire alight.*
- *Is it mad you are?*
- *It's childless you'd be to this day if you hadn't turned to me.*

3 The story is written from Owen's point of view and the author often puts Owen's thoughts in question-form, for example:

> *Why bother with gloves at all? This was his own cottage, wasn't it?*

This could be rewritten as:

> He decided there was no need to bother with gloves because it was his own cottage.

Find some other examples and rewrite them in the same way, as simple description of Owen's thoughts. Then compare the different versions. What effect do the questions have? Do they contribute to the tension of the story, or our understanding of Owen's character?

ACTIVITIES

1 Write a report of the tragedy for the local newspaper, including interviews with Mrs Price and Ma Hughes, who both guess (rightly or wrongly) at reasons for Owen's death.

2 Imagine that when Owen entered his cottage, he discovered that only Beth the dog was dead, and not Margo as well. Write a new ending for the story. How does Owen explain Beth's death to Margo? Does he make another attempt to murder Huw?

3 The title of the story, *Ricochet*, suggests the unexpected ending, or the miscarriage of Owen's plan; as Shakespeare put it, 'purposes mistook / Fallen on the inventors' heads.' Think of some other titles for the story, perhaps associated with Owen's emotions, or the animals in the story, or the Welsh countryside.

THE FOUNTAIN PLAYS

THE AUTHOR

Dorothy L. Sayers was born in 1893. She received a classical education and was one of the first women to obtain a degree from Oxford University. She worked in an advertising agency for ten years and led a flamboyant and unconventional life, achieving early fame as a writer of skilfully plotted detective novels. Many of these feature her most popular character, Lord Peter Wimsey, a charming, intelligent aristocrat and amateur detective. Her best-known stories include *Have His Carcase*, *Strong Poison*, *Gaudy Night*, *The Nine Tailors* (an ingenious plot involving the complexities of church bell-ringing), and *Murder Must Advertise* (set in the advertising world). She died in 1957.

THE STORY

Some people have a skeleton in the cupboard, a secret which, if revealed, would be embarrassing, or worse. It depends, of course, on the nature of the secret as to how far someone will go to keep it hidden. A little harmless deception, being 'economical with the truth', outright lies? But what if another person already knows? What if they threaten to tell? Being blackmailed is a most unpleasant experience, but perhaps it is the lesser of two evils.

Mr Spiller has just installed an ornamental fountain in his garden. He is rather proud of it, and takes his dinner guests out to admire it. His neighbour Mrs Digby is enthusiastic, his future son-in-law mildly sarcastic, and Mr Gooch disagreeably offensive. In fact, Mr Gooch's behaviour strikes the only jarring note in an otherwise pleasant evening . . .

THE FOUNTAIN PLAYS

'Yes,' said Mr Spiller, in a satisfied tone, 'I must say I like a bit of ornamental water. Gives a finish to the place.'

'The Versailles* touch,' agreed Ronald Proudfoot.

Mr Spiller glanced sharply at him, as though suspecting sarcasm, but his lean face expressed nothing whatsoever. Mr Spiller was never quite at his ease in the company of his daughter's fiancé, though he was proud of the girl's achievement. With all his (to Mr Spiller) unamiable qualities, Ronald Proudfoot was a perfect gentleman, and Betty was completely wrapped up in him.

'The only thing it wants,' continued Mr Spiller, 'to *my* mind, that is, is Opening Up. To make a Vista, so to say. You don't get the Effect with these bushes on all four sides.'

'Oh, I don't know, Mr Spiller,' objected Mrs Digby in her mild voice. 'Don't you think it makes rather a fascinating surprise? You come along the path, never dreaming there's anything behind those lilacs, and then you turn the corner and come suddenly upon it. I'm sure, when you brought me down to see it this afternoon, it quite took my breath away.'

'There's that, of course,' admitted Mr Spiller. It occurred to him, not for the first time, that there was something very attractive about Mrs Digby's silvery personality. She had distinction, too. A widow and widower of the sensible time of life, with a bit of money on both sides, might do worse than settle down comfortably in a pleasant house with half an acre of garden and a bit of ornamental water.

'And it's so pretty and secluded,' went on Mrs Digby, 'with these glorious rhododendrons. Look how pretty they are, all sprayed with the water – like fairy jewels – and the rustic seat against those dark cypresses at the back. Really Italian. And the scent of the lilac is so marvellous!'

Mr Spiller knew that the cypresses were, in fact, yews, but he did not correct her. A little ignorance was becoming in a woman. He glanced from the cotoneasters at one side of the fountain to the rhododendrons on the other, their rainbow flower-trusses sparkling with diamond drops.

'I wasn't thinking of touching the rhododendrons or the cotoneasters,' he said. 'I only thought of cutting through that great hedge of lilac, so as to make a vista from the house. But the ladies must always have the last word, mustn't they – er – Ronald?' (He never could bring out Proudfoot's Christian name naturally.) 'If you like it as it is, Mrs Digby, that settles it. The lilacs shall stay.'

'It's too flattering of you,' said Mrs Digby, 'but you mustn't think of altering your plans for me. I haven't any right to interfere with your beautiful garden.'

'Indeed you have,' said Mr Spiller. 'I defer to your taste entirely. You have spoken for the lilacs, and henceforward they are sacred.'

'I shall be afraid to give an opinion on anything, after that,' said Mrs Digby, shaking her head. 'But whatever you decide to do, I'm sure it will be lovely. It was a marvellous idea to think of putting the fountain there. It makes all the difference to the garden.'

Mr Spiller thought she was quite right. And indeed, though the fountain was rather flattered by the name of 'ornamental water', consisting as it did of a marble basin set in the centre of a pool about four feet square, it made a brave show, with its plume of dancing water, fifteen feet high, towering over the smaller shrubs and almost overtopping the tall lilacs. And its cooling splash and tinkle soothed the ear on this pleasant day of early summer.

'Costs a bit to run, doesn't it?' demanded Mr Gooch. He had been silent up till now, and Mrs Digby felt that his remark betrayed a rather sordid outlook on life. Indeed, from the first moment of meeting Mr Gooch, she had pronounced him decidedly common, and wondered that he should be on such intimate terms with her host.

'No, no,' replied Mr Spiller. 'No, it's not expensive. You see, it uses the same water over and over again. Most ingenious. The fountains in Trafalgar Square* work on the same principle, I believe. Of course, I had to pay a bit to have it put in, but I think it's worth the money.'

'Yes, indeed,' said Mrs Digby

'I always said you were a warm man*, Spiller,' said Mr Gooch, with his vulgar laugh. 'Wish I was in your shoes. A snug spot, that's what I call this place. Snug.'

'I'm not a millionaire,' answered Mr Spiller, rather shortly. 'But things might be worse in these times. Of course,' he added, more cheerfully, 'one has to be careful. I turn the fountain off at night, for instance, to save leakage and waste.'

'I'll swear you do, you damned old miser,' said Mr Gooch offensively.

Mr Spiller was saved replying by the sounding of a gong in the distance.

'Ah! there's dinner,' he announced, with a certain relief in his tone. The party wound their way out between the lilacs, and paced gently up the long crazy pavement, past the herbaceous borders and the two long beds of raw little ticketed roses, to the glorified villa which Mr Spiller had christened 'The Pleasaunce'.

It seemed to Mrs Digby that there was a slightly strained atmosphere about dinner, though Betty, pretty as a picture and very much in love with Ronald Proudfoot, made a perfectly charming little hostess. The jarring note was sounded by Mr Gooch. He ate too noisily, drank far too freely, got on Proudfoot's nerves and behaved to Mr Spiller with a kind of veiled insolence which was embarrassing and disagreeable to listen to. She wondered again where he had come from, and why Mr Spiller put up with him. She knew little about him, except that from time to time he turned up on a visit to 'The Pleasaunce', usually staying there about a month and being, apparently, well supplied with cash. She had an idea that he was some kind of commission agent, though she could not recall any distinct statement on this point. Mr Spiller had settled down in the village about three years previously, and she had always liked him. Though not, in any sense of the word, a cultivated man, he was kind, generous and unassuming, and his devotion to Betty had something very lovable about it. Mr Gooch had started coming about a year later. Mrs Digby said to herself that if ever she was in a position to lay down the law at 'The Pleasaunce' – and she had begun to think matters were tending that way – her influence would be directed to getting rid of Mr Gooch.

'How about a spot of bridge?' suggested Ronald Proudfoot, when coffee had been served. It was nice, reflected Mrs Digby, to have coffee brought in by the manservant. Masters was really a very well-trained butler, though he did combine the office with that of chauffeur. One would be comfortable at 'The Pleasaunce'. From the dining-room window she could see the neat garage housing the Wolseley saloon on the ground floor, with a room for the chauffeur above it, and topped off by a handsome gilded weather-vane a-glitter in the last rays of the sun. A good cook, a smart parlourmaid and everything done exactly as one could wish – if she were to marry Mr Spiller she would be able, for the first time in her life, to afford a personal maid as well. There would be plenty of room in the house, and of course, when Betty was married –

Betty, she thought, was not over-pleased that Ronald had suggested bridge. Bridge is not a game that lends itself to the expression of tender feeling, and it would perhaps have looked better if Ronald had enticed Betty out to sit in the lilac-scented dusk under the yew-hedge by the fountain. Mrs Digby was sometimes afraid that Betty was the more in love of the two. But if Ronald wanted anything he had to have it, of course, and personally, Mrs Digby enjoyed nothing better than a quiet rubber. Besides, the arrangement had the advantage that it got rid of Mr Gooch. 'Don't play bridge,' Mr Gooch was wont to say. 'Never had time to learn. We didn't play bridge where I was brought up.' He repeated the remark now, and followed it up with a contemptuous snort directed at Mr Spiller.

'Never too late to begin,' said the latter pacifically.

'Not me!' retorted Mr Gooch. 'I'm going to have a turn in the garden. Where's that fellow Masters? Tell him to take the whisky and soda down to the fountain. The decanter, mind – one drink's no good to yours truly*.' He plunged a thick hand into the box of Coronas on the side-table, took out a handful of cigars and passed out through the French window of the library on to the terrace. Mr Spiller rang the bell and gave the order without comment, and presently they saw Masters pad down the long crazy path between the rose-beds and the herbaceous borders, bearing the whisky and soda on a tray.

The other four played on till 10.30, when a rubber coming to an end, Mrs Digby rose and said it was time she went home. Her host gallantly offered to accompany her. 'These two young people can look after themselves for a moment,' he added, with a conspiratorial smile.

'The young can look after themselves better than the old, these days.' She laughed a little shyly, and raised no objection when Mr Spiller drew her hand into his arm as they walked the couple of hundred yards to her cottage. She hesitated a moment whether to ask him in, but decided that a sweet decorum suited her style best.

She stretched out a soft, beringed hand to him over the top of the little white gate. His pressure lingered – he would have kissed the hand, so insidious was the scent of the red and white hawthorns in her trim garden, but before he had summoned up the courage, she had withdrawn it from his clasp and was gone.

Mr Spiller, opening his own front door in an agreeable dream, encountered Masters.

'Where is everybody, Masters?'

'Mr Proudfoot left five or ten minutes since, sir, and Miss Elizabeth has retired.'

'Oh!' Mr Spiller was a little startled. The new generation, he thought sadly, did not make love like the old. He hoped there was nothing wrong. Another irritating thought presented itself.

'Has Mr Gooch come in?'

'I could not say, sir. Shall I go and see?'

'No, never mind.' If Gooch had been sozzling himself up with whisky since dinner-time, it was just as well Masters should keep away from him. You never knew. Masters was one of these soft-spoken beggars, but he might take advantage. Better not to trust servants, anyhow.

'You can cut along to bed. I'll lock up.'

'Very good, sir.'

'Oh, by the way, is the fountain turned off?'

'Yes, sir. I turned it off myself, sir, at half-past ten, seeing that you were engaged, sir.'

'Quite right. Good-night, Masters.'

'Good-night, sir.'

He heard the man go out by the back and cross the paved court to the garage. Thoughtfully he bolted both entrances; and returned to the library. The whisky decanter was not in its usual place – no doubt it was still with Gooch in the garden – but he mixed himself a small brandy and soda, and drank it. He supposed he must now face the tiresome business of getting Gooch up to bed. Then, suddenly, he realized that the encounter would take place here and not in the garden. Gooch was coming in through the French window. He was drunk, but not, Mr Spiller observed with relief, incapably so.

'Well?' said Gooch.

'Well?' retorted Mr Spiller.

'Had a good time with the accommodating widow, eh? Enjoyed yourself? Lucky old hound, aren't you? Fallen soft in your old age, eh?'

'There, that'll do,' said Mr Spiller.

'Oh, will it? That's good. That's rich. That'll do, eh? Think I'm Masters, talking to me like that?' Mr Gooch gave a thick chuckle. 'Well, I'm not Masters, I'm master here. Get that into your head. I'm master and you damn well know it.'

'All right,' replied Mr Spiller meekly, 'but buzz off to bed now, there's a good fellow. It's getting late and I'm tired.'

'You'll be tireder before I've done with you.' Mr Gooch thrust both hands into his pockets and stood – a bulky and threatening figure – swaying rather dangerously. 'I'm short of cash,' he added. 'Had a bad week – cleaned me out. Time you stumped up a bit more.'

'Nonsense,' said Mr Spiller, with some spirit. 'I pay you your allowance as we agreed, and let you come and stay here whenever you like, and that's all you get from me.'

'Oh, is it? Getting a bit above yourself, aren't you, Number Bleeding 4132?'

'Hush!' said Mr Spiller, glancing hastily round as though the furniture had ears and tongues.

'Hush! hush!' repeated Mr Gooch mockingly. 'You're in a good position to dictate terms, aren't you, 4132? Hush! The servants might hear! Betty might hear! Betty's young man might hear. Hah!

Betty's young man – he'd be particularly pleased to know her father was an escaped jail-bird, wouldn't he? Liable at any moment to be hauled back to work out his ten years' hard* for forgery? And when I think,' added Mr Gooch, 'that a man like me, that was only in for a short stretch and worked it out good and proper, is dependent on the charity – ha, ha! – of my dear friend 4132, while he's rolling in wealth –'

'I'm not rolling in wealth, Sam,' said Mr Spiller, 'and you know darn well I'm not. But I don't want any trouble. I'll do what I can, if you'll promise faithfully this time that you won't ask for any more of these big sums, because my income won't stand it.'

'Oh, I'll promise that all right,' agreed Mr Gooch cheerfully. 'You give me five thousand down –'

Mr Spiller uttered a strangled exclamation.

'Five thousand? How do you suppose I'm to lay hands on five thousand all at once? Don't be an idiot, Sam. I'll give you a cheque for five hundred –'

'Five thousand,' insisted Mr Gooch, 'or up goes the monkey.'

'But I haven't got it,' objected Mr Spiller.

'Then you'd bloody well better find it,' returned Mr Gooch.

'How do you expect me to find all that?'

'That's your look-out. You oughtn't to be so damned extravagant. Spending good money, that you ought to be giving *me*, on fountains and stuff. Now, it's no good kicking, Mr Respectable 4132 – I'm the man on top and you're for it, my lad, if you don't look after me properly. See?'

Mr Spiller saw it only too clearly. He saw, as he had seen indeed for some time, that his friend Gooch had him by the short hairs. He expostulated again feebly, and Gooch replied with a laugh and an offensive reference to Mrs Digby.

Mr Spiller did not realize that he had struck very hard. He hardly

realized that he had struck at all. He thought he had aimed a
blow, and that Gooch had dodged it and tripped over the leg of
the occasional table. But he was not very clear in his mind, except
on one point. Gooch was dead.

He had not fainted; he was not stunned. He was dead. He must
have caught the brass curb of the fender as he fell. There was no
blood, but Mr Spiller, exploring the inert head with anxious
fingers, found a spot above the temple where the bone yielded to
pressure like a cracked egg-shell. The noise of the fall had been
thunderous. Kneeling there on the library floor, Mr Spiller waited
for the inevitable cry and footsteps from upstairs.

Nothing happened. He remembered – with difficulty, for his
mind seemed to be working slowly and stiffly – that above the
library there was only the long drawing-room, and over that the
spare-room and bathrooms. No inhabited bedroom looked out on
that side of the house.

A slow, grinding, grating noise startled him. He whisked round
hastily. The old-fashioned grandfather clock, wheezing as the
hammer rose into action, struck eleven. He wiped the sweat from
his forehead, got up and poured himself out another, and a stiffer,
brandy.

The drink did him good. It seemed to take the brake off his
mind, and the wheels span energetically. An extraordinary clarity
took the place of his previous confusion.

He had murdered Gooch. He had not exactly intended to do
so, but he had done it. It had not felt to him like murder, but
there was not the slightest doubt what the police would think
about it. And once he was in the hands of the police – Mr Spiller
shuddered. They would almost certainly want to take his
finger-prints, and would be surprised to recognize a bunch of old
friends.

Masters had heard him say that he would wait up for Gooch.

Masters knew that everybody else had gone to bed. Masters would undoubtedly guess something. But stop!

Could Masters prove that he himself had gone to bed? Yes, probably he could. Somebody would have heard him cross the court and seen the light go up over the garage. One could not hope to throw suspicion on Masters – besides, the man hardly deserved that. But the mere idea had started Mr Spiller's brain on a new and attractive line of thought.

What he really wanted was an alibi. If he could only confuse the police as to the time at which Gooch had died. If Gooch could be made to seem alive after he was dead . . . somehow . . .

He cast his thoughts back over stories he had read on holiday, dealing with this very matter. You dressed up as the dead man and impersonated him. You telephoned in his name. In the hearing of the butler, you spoke to the dead man as though he were alive. You made a gramophone record of his voice and played it. You hid the body, and thereafter sent a forged letter from some distant place –

He paused for a moment. Forgery – but he did not want to start that old game over again. And all these things were too elaborate, or else impracticable at that time of night.

And then it came to him suddenly that he was a fool. Gooch must not be made to live later, but to die earlier. He should die before 10.30, at the time when Mr Spiller, under the eyes of three observers, had been playing bridge.

So far, the idea was sound and even, in its broad outline, obvious. But now one had to come down to detail. How could he establish the time? Was there anything that had happened at 10.30?

He helped himself to another drink, and then, quite suddenly, as though lit by a floodlight, he saw his whole plan, picked out vividly, complete, with every join and angle clear-cut.

He glanced at his watch; the hands stood at twenty minutes past eleven. He had the night before him.

He fetched an electric torch from the hall and stepped boldly out of the French window. Close beside it, against the wall of the house, were two taps, one ending in a nozzle for the garden hose, the other controlling the fountain at the bottom of the garden. This latter he turned on, and then, without troubling to muffle his footsteps, followed the crazy-paved path down to the lilac hedge, and round by the bed of the cotoneasters. The sky, despite the beauty of the early evening, had now turned very dark, and he could scarcely see the tall column of pale water above the dark shrubbery, but he heard its comforting splash and ripple, and as he stepped upon the surrounding grass he felt the blown spray upon his face. The beam of the torch showed him the garden seat beneath the yews, and the tray, as he had expected, standing upon it. The whisky decanter was about half full. He emptied the greater part of its contents into the basin, wrapping the neck of the decanter in his handkerchief, so as to leave no fingerprints. Then, returning to the other side of the lilacs, he satisfied himself that the spray of the fountain was invisible from house or garden.

The next part of the performance he did not care about. It was risky; it might be heard; in fact, he wanted it to be heard if necessary – but it was a risk. He licked his dry lips and called the dead man by name:

'Gooch! Gooch!'

No answer, except the splash of the fountain, sounding to his anxious ear abnormally loud in the stillness. He glanced round, almost as though he expected the corpse to stalk awfully out upon him from the darkness, its head hanging and its dark mouth dropping open to show the pale gleam of its dentures. Then, pulling himself together, he walked briskly back up the path and, when he reached the house again, listened. There was no movement, no sound but the ticking of the clock. He shut the library door gently. From now on there must be no noise.

There was a pair of galoshes in the cloak-room near the pantry. He put them on and slipped like a shadow through the French window again; then round the house into the courtyard. He glanced up at the garage; there was no light in the upper story and he breathed a sigh of relief, for Masters was apt sometimes to be wakeful. Groping his way to an outhouse, he switched the torch on. His wife had been an invalid for some years before her death, and he had brought her wheeled chair with him to 'The Pleasaunce', having a dim, sentimental reluctance to sell the thing. He was thankful for that, now; thankful, too, that he had purchased it from a good maker and that it ran so lightly and silently on its pneumatic tyres. He found the bicycle pump and blew the tyres up hard and, for further precaution, administered a drop of oil here and there. Then, with infinite precaution, he wheeled the chair round to the library window. How fortunate that he had put down stone flags and crazy paving everywhere, so that no wheel-tracks could show.

The job of getting the body through the window and into the chair took it out of him. Gooch had been a heavy man, and he himself was not in good training. But it was done at last. Resisting the impulse to run, he pushed his burden gently and steadily along the narrow strip of paving. He could not see very well, and he was afraid to flash his torch too often. A slip off the path into the herbaceous border would be fatal; he set his teeth and kept his gaze fixed steadily ahead of him. He felt as though, if he looked back at the house, he would see the upper windows thronged with staring white faces. The impulse to turn his head was almost irresistible, but he determined that he would not turn it.

At length he was round the edge of the lilacs and hidden from the house. The sweat was running down his face and the most ticklish part of his task was still to do. If he broke his heart in the effort, he must carry the body over the plot of lawn. No wheel-marks or heel-marks or signs of dragging must be left for the police to see. He braced himself for the effort.

It was done. The corpse of Gooch lay there by the fountain, the bruise upon the temple carefully adjusted upon the sharp stone edge of the pool, one hand dragging in the water, the limbs disposed as naturally as possible, to look as though the man had stumbled and fallen. Over it, from head to foot, the water of the fountain sprayed, swaying and bending in the night wind. Mr Spiller looked upon his work and saw that it was good. The journey back with the lightened chair was easy. When he had returned the vehicle to the outhouse and passed for the last time through the library window, he felt as though the burden of years had been rolled from his back.

His back! He had remembered to take off his dinner-jacket while stooping in the spray of the fountain, and only his shirt was drenched. That he could dispose of in the linen-basket, but the seat of his trousers gave him some uneasiness. He mopped at himself as best he could with his handkerchief. Then he made his calculations. If he left the fountain to play for an hour or so it would, he thought, produce the desired effect. Controlling his devouring impatience, he sat down and mixed himself a final brandy.

At one o'clock he rose, turned off the fountain, shut the library window with no more and no less than the usual noise and force, and went with firm footsteps up to bed.

Inspector Frampton was, to Mr Spiller's delight, a highly intelligent officer. He picked up the clues thrown to him with the eagerness of a trained terrier. The dead man was last seen alive by Masters after dinner – 8.30 – just so. After which, the rest of the party had played bridge together till 10.30. Mr Spiller had then gone out with Mrs Digby. Just after he left, Masters had turned off the fountain. Mr Proudfoot had left at 10.40 and Miss Spiller and the maids had then retired. Mr Spiller had come in again at 10.45 or 10.50, and inquired for Mr Gooch. After this, Masters had gone across to the garage, leaving Mr Spiller to lock up. Later on, Mr Spiller had gone down the garden to look for Mr Gooch. He had gone no farther than the lilac hedge, and there calling to him and getting no answer, had concluded that his guest had already come in and gone to bed. The housemaid fancied she had heard him calling Mr Gooch. She placed this episode at about half-past eleven – certainly not later. Mr Spiller had subsequently sat up reading in the library till one o'clock, when he had shut the window and gone to bed also.

The body, when found by the gardener at 6.30 a.m., was still wet with the spray from the fountain, which had also soaked the grass beneath it. Since the fountain had been turned off at 10.30, this meant that Gooch must have lain there for an appreciable period before that. In view of the large quantity of whisky that he had drunk, it seemed probable that he had had a heart-attack, or had drunkenly stumbled, and, in falling, had struck his head on the edge of the pool. All these considerations fixed the time of death at from 9.30 to 10 o'clock – an opinion with which the doctor, though declining to commit himself within an hour or so, concurred, and the coroner entered a verdict of accidental death.

Only the man who has been for years the helpless victim of blackmail could fully enter into Mr Spiller's feelings. Compunction played no part in them – the relief was far too great. To be rid of the daily irritation of Gooch's presence, of his insatiable demands for money, of the perpetual menace of his drunken malice – these boons were well worth a murder. And,

Mr Spiller insisted to himself as he sat musing on the rustic seat by the fountain, it had not really been murder. He determined to call on Mrs Digby that afternoon. He could ask her to marry him now without haunting fear for the future. The scent of the lilac was intoxicating.

'Excuse me, sir,' said Masters.

Mr Spiller, withdrawing his meditative gaze from the spouting water, looked inquiringly at the man-servant, who stood in a respectful attitude beside him.

'If it is convenient to you, sir, I should wish to have my bedroom changed. I should wish to sleep indoors.'

'Oh?' said Mr Spiller. 'Why that, Masters?'

'I am subject to be a light sleeper, sir, ever since the war, and I find the creaking of the weather-vane very disturbing.'

'It creaks, does it?'

'Yes, sir. On the night that Mr Gooch sustained his unfortunate accident, sir, the wind changed at a quarter past eleven. The creaking woke me out of my first sleep, sir, and disturbed me very much.'

A coldness gripped Mr Spiller at the pit of the stomach. The servant's eyes, in that moment, reminded him curiously of Gooch. He had never noticed any resemblance before.

'It's a curious thing, sir, if I may say so, that, with the wind shifting as it did at 11.15, Mr Gooch's body should have become sprayed by the fountain. Up till 11.15 the spray was falling on the other side, sir. The appearance presented was as though the body had been placed in position subsequently to 11.15, sir, and the fountain turned on again.'

'Very strange,' said Mr Spiller. On the other side of the lilac hedge, he heard the voices of Betty and Ronald Proudfoot, chattering as they paced to and fro between the herbaceous borders. They seemed to be happy together. The whole house seemed happier, now that Gooch was gone.

'Very strange indeed, sir. I may add that, after hearing the inspector's observations, I took the precaution to dry your dress-trousers in the linen-cupboard in the bathroom.'

'Oh, yes,' said Mr Spiller.

'I shall not, of course, mention the change of wind to the authorities, sir, and now that the inquest is over, it is not likely to occur to anybody, unless their attention should be drawn to it. I think, sir, all things being taken into consideration, you might find it worth your while to retain me permanently in your service at – shall we say double my present wage to begin with?'

Mr Spiller opened his mouth to say, 'Go to Hell,' but his voice failed him. He bowed his head.

'I am much obliged to you, sir,' said Masters, and withdrew on silent feet.

Mr Spiller looked at the fountain, with its tall water wavering and bending in the wind.

'Ingenious,' he muttered automatically, 'and it really costs nothing to run. It uses the same water over and over again.'

NOTES

Versailles (p69)
Louis XIV's palace at Versailles near Paris, famous for its gardens and fountains
Trafalgar Square (p71)
a famous square in London, with large fountains
a warm man (p71)
a man who is comfortably settled; rich, affluent (now rarely used)
yours truly (p73)
a formal phrase used to sign off a letter, and (as here) used in a colloquial way to mean 'me' or 'myself'
ten years' hard (p76)
short for ten years' hard labour: imprisonment with heavy physical work as a punishment

DISCUSSION

1   Why do you think Mr Spiller allows himself to be blackmailed, first by Gooch and then by Masters? What would you have done in his position?

2   If Gooch had not died, do you think Mr Spiller could have married Mrs Digby? Imagine that Mr Spiller has proposed to Mrs Digby and been accepted. How might Gooch respond to this?

3   Mr Spiller, Mr Gooch, and Mrs Digby all have different attitudes towards money. Can you describe the differences?

4   Can you explain the significance of the last line of the story?

LANGUAGE FOCUS

1   What do these expressions mean, in the context in which they are used in the story? Rephrase them in your own words.

   it quite took my breath away (p69)
   You can cut along to bed. (p74)
   That's rich. (p75)
   Had a bad week – cleaned me out. (p75)
   Time you stumped up a bit more. (p75)

> *Getting a bit above yourself, aren't you?* (p75)
> *I'm not rolling in wealth.* (p76)
> *or up goes the monkey* (p76)
> *That's your look-out.* (p76)
> *I'm the man on top and you're for it* (p76)
> *Gooch had him by the short hairs.* (p76)

2   Find the places in the story where Gooch and Masters make threats
    to Mr Spiller. In both cases the message is quite clear, but the two
    blackmailers use very different language. Gooch is crude and direct,
    informal to the point of rudeness; Masters uses polite, formal language,
    appropriate for a servant speaking to an employer. Rewrite the main
    message of each man's threats, in the other's style. You might begin
    like this:

> Gooch: *May I suggest five thousand? Otherwise, I fear I shall have
> to* . . .
> Masters: *I'll keep my mouth shut, Spiller, about the change of wind,
> and nobody's going to* . . .

ACTIVITIES

1   What do you think might happen after the end of the story? Will Mr
    Spiller be able to marry Mrs Digby? Or will Masters prevent him from
    doing so? Will Mr Spiller find it necessary to kill Masters? Write a
    further final paragraph describing what happens to these three
    characters.

2   Imagine that Mr Spiller refuses to be blackmailed by Masters, who
    gives his information to the police. Mr Spiller is arrested for Gooch's
    murder. Write the speech for the defence at his trial.

THREE IS A LUCKY NUMBER

THE AUTHOR

Margery Allingham was born in 1904. She came from a family of writers, and was trained to be a writer by her father from the age of seven. *The Crime at Black Dudley* was her first story about the amateur detective who was to become her most famous character, Albert Campion, a mild-mannered man with glasses. She wrote more than twenty novels and many short stories. Among her earlier, more light-hearted titles are *More Work for the Undertaker*, *Flowers for the Judge*, and *Death of a Ghost*. Her later novels, such as *The Tiger in the Smoke* and *Hide My Eyes*, show more psychological analysis and detailed characterization. She died in 1966.

THE STORY

Is there such a thing as the 'perfect' murder? A murder that is so skilfully planned and executed that there is no possibility of the murderer ever being caught? Many crime writers explore this idea. Sometimes the murderer gets away with it; sometimes it is only the flaws in his own character that lead to his undoing – his vanity or his wish to boast, perhaps, or his conceit.

Ronald Torbay has a rather curious way of earning a living, or rather, acquiring an income. However, he is thorough and meticulous in the pursuit of his chosen career. His wife, Edyth, is essential to his plans, but she, of course, is far too stupid to understand the beautiful simplicity of his system . . .

THREE IS A LUCKY NUMBER

At five o'clock on a September afternoon Ronald Frederick Torbay was making preparations for his third murder. He was being very wary, forcing himself to go slowly because he was perfectly sane and was well aware of the dangers of carelessness.

A career of homicide got more chancy as one went on. That piece of information had impressed him as being true as soon as he had read it in a magazine article way back before his first marriage. Also, he realized, success was liable to go to a man's head, so he kept a tight hold on himself. He was certain he was infinitely more clever than most human beings but he did not dwell on the fact and as soon as he felt the old thrill at the sense of his power welling up inside him, he quelled it firmly.

For an instant he paused, leaning on the rim of the wash-basin, and regarded himself thoughtfully in the shaving glass of the bathroom in the new villa he had hired so recently.

The face which looked at him was thin, middle-aged, and pallid. Sparse dark hair receded from its high narrow forehead and the well-shaped eyes were blue and prominent. Only the mouth was really unusual. That narrow slit, quite straight, was almost lipless and, unconsciously, he persuaded it to relax into a half smile. Even Ronald Torbay did not like his own mouth.

A sound in the kitchen below disturbed him and he straightened his back hastily. If Edyth had finished her ironing she would be coming up to take her long discussed bubble-bath before he had prepared it for her and that would never do. He waited, holding his breath, but it was all right: she was going out of the back door. He reached the window just in time to see her disappearing round the side of the house into the small square yard which was so exactly like all the other square yards in the long suburban street.

He knew that she was going to hang the newly pressed linen on the line to air and although the manoeuvre gave him the time he needed, still it irritated him.

Of the three homely middle-aged women whom so far he had persuaded first to marry him and then to will him their modest possessions, Edyth was proving easily the most annoying. If he had told her once not to spend so much time in the yard he had done it a dozen times in their six weeks of marriage. He hated her being out of doors alone. She was shy and reserved but now that new people had moved in next door there was the danger of some over-friendly woman starting up an acquaintance with her and that was the last thing to be tolerated at this juncture.

Each of his former wives had been shy. He had been very careful to choose the right type and felt he owed much of his success to it. Mary, the first of them, had met her fatal 'accident' almost unnoticed in the bungalow on the housing estate very like the present one he had chosen but in the north instead of the south of England. At the time it had been a growing place, the coroner had been hurried, the police sympathetic but busy and the neighbours scarcely curious except that one of them, a junior reporter on a local paper, had written a flowery paragraph about the nearness of tragedy in the midst of joy, published a wedding day snapshot and had entitled the article with typical northern understatement 'Honeymoon Mishap'.

Dorothy's brief excursion into his life and abrupt exit from it and her own, had given him a little more bother but not much. She had deceived him when she had told him she was quite alone in the world and the interfering brother who had turned up after the funeral to ask awkward questions about her small fortune might have been a nuisance if Ronald had not been very firm with him. There had been a brief court case which Ronald had won handsomely and the insurance had paid up without a murmur.

All that was four years ago. Now, with a new name, a newly invented background and a fresh area in which to operate, he felt remarkably safe.

From the moment he had first seen Edyth, sitting alone at a little table under the window in a seaside hotel dining-room, he had known that she was to be his next subject. He always thought of his wives as 'subjects'. It lent his designs upon them a certain pseudo-scientific atmosphere which he found satisfying.

Edyth had sat there looking stiff and neat and a trifle severe but there had been a secret timidity in her face, an unsatisfied, half-frightened expression in her short-sighted eyes and once, when the waiter said something pleasant to her, she had flushed nervously and had been embarrassed by it. She was also wearing a genuine diamond brooch. Ronald had observed that from right across the room. He had an eye for stones.

That evening in the lounge he had spoken to her, had weathered the initial snub, tried again and, finally, had got her to talk. After that the acquaintance had progressed just as he had expected. His methods were old-fashioned and heavily romantic and within a week she was hopelessly infatuated.

From Ronald's point of view her history was even better than he could have hoped. After teaching in a girls' boarding school for the whole of her twenties she had been summoned home to look after her recluse of a father whose long illness had monopolized her life. Now at forty-three she was alone, comparatively well off and as much at sea as a ship without a rudder.

Ronald was careful not to let her toes touch the ground. He devoted his entire attention to her and exactly five weeks from the day on which they first met, he married her at the registry office of the town where they were both strangers. The same afternoon they each made wills in the other's favour and moved into the villa which he had been able to hire cheaply because the holiday season was at an end.

It had been the pleasantest conquest he had ever made. Mary had been moody and hysterical, Dorothy grudging and suspicious but Edyth had revealed an unexpected streak of gaiety and, but for her stupidity in not realizing that a man would hardly fall romantically in love with her at first sight, was a sensible person. Any other man, Ronald reflected smugly, might have made the fatal mistake of feeling sorry for her, but he was 'above' all that, he told himself, and he began to make plans for what he described in his own mind rather grimly as 'her future'.

Two things signed her death warrant earlier than had been his original intention. One was her obstinate reticence over her monetary affairs and the other was her embarrassing interest in his job.

On the marriage certificate Ronald had described himself as a salesman and the story he was telling was that he was a junior partner in a firm of cosmetic manufacturers who were giving him a very generous leave of absence. Edyth accepted the statement without question, but almost at once she had begun to plan a visit to the office and the factory, and was always talking about the new clothes she must buy so as not to 'disgrace him'. At the same time she kept all her business papers locked in an old writing-case and steadfastly refused to discuss them however cautiously he raised the subject. Ronald had given up feeling angry with her and decided to act.

He turned from the window, carefully removed his jacket and began to run the bath. His heart was pounding, he noticed, frowning. He wished it would not. He needed to keep very calm.

The bathroom was the one room they had repainted. Ronald had done it himself soon after they had arrived and had put up the little shelf over the bath to hold a jar of bathsalts he had bought and a small electric heater of the old-fashioned two-element type, which was cheap but white like the walls and not too noticeable. He leant forward now and switched it on and stood looking at it until the two bars of glowing warmth appeared. Then he turned away and went out on to the landing, leaving it alight.

The fuse box which controlled all the electricity in the house was concealed in the bottom of the linen cupboard at the top of the stairs. Ronald opened the door carefully and using his handkerchief so that his fingerprints should leave no trace pulled up the main switch. Back in the bathroom the heater's glow died away; the bars were almost black again by the time he returned. He eyed the slender cabinet approvingly and then, still using the handkerchief, he lifted it bodily from the shelf and lowered it carefully into the water, arranging it so that it lay at an angle over the waste plug, close to the foot where it took up practically no room at all. The white flex ran up over the porcelain side of the bath, along the skirting board, under the door and into the wall socket, just outside on the landing.

When he had first installed the heater Edyth had demurred at this somewhat slipshod arrangement, but when he had explained that the local Council* was stupid and fussy about fitting wall sockets in bathrooms since water was said to be a conductor she had compromised by letting him run the flex under the lino where it was not so noticeable.

At the moment the heater was perfectly visible in the bath. It certainly looked as if it had fallen into its odd position accidentally but no one in his senses could have stepped into the water without seeing it. Ronald paused, his eyes dark, his ugly mouth narrower than ever. The beautiful simplicity of the main plan, so certain, so swiftly fatal and above all, so safe as far as he himself was concerned gave him a thrill of pleasure as it always did. He turned off the bath and waited, listening. Edyth was coming back. He could hear her moving something on the concrete way outside the back door below and he leant over to where his jacket hung and took a plastic sachet from its inside breast pocket. He was re-reading the directions on the back of it when a slight sound made him turn his head and he saw, to his horror, the woman herself not five feet away. Her neat head had appeared suddenly just above the flat roof of the scullery, outside the bathroom window. She was clearing the dead leaves from the guttering and must, he guessed, be standing on the tall flight of steps which were kept just inside the back door.

It was typical of the man that he did not panic. Still holding the sachet lightly he stepped between her and the bath and spoke mildly.

'What on earth are you doing there, darling?'

Edyth started so violently at the sound of his voice that she almost fell off the steps and a flush of apprehension appeared on her thin cheeks.

'Oh, how you startled me! I thought I'd just do this little job before I came up to change. If it rains the gutter floods all over the back step.'

'Very thoughtful of you, my dear.' He spoke with that slightly acid amusement with which he had found he could best destroy her slender vein of self-assurance. 'But not terribly clever when you knew I'd come up to prepare your beauty bath for you. Or was it?'

The slight intonation on the word 'beauty' was not lost on her. He saw her swallow.

'Perhaps it wasn't,' she said without looking at him. 'It's very good of you to take all this trouble, Ronald.'

'Not at all,' he said with a just amount of masculine, offhand insensitivity. 'I'm taking you out tonight and I want you to look as nice as – er – possible. Hurry up, there's a good girl. The foam doesn't last indefinitely and like all these very high-class beauty treatments the ingredients are expensive. Undress in the bedroom, put on your gown and come straight along.'

'Very well, dear.' She began to descend at once while he turned to the bath and shook the contents of the sachet into the water. The crystals, which were peach coloured and smelled strongly of roses, floated on the tide and then, as he suddenly turned the pressure of water full on, began to dissolve into thousands of irridescent bubbles. A momentary fear that their camouflage would not prove to be sufficient assailed him, and he stooped to beat the water with his hand, but he need not have worried. The cloud grew and grew into a fragrant feathery mass which not only obscured the bottom of the bath and all it contained, but mounted the porcelain side, smothering the white flex and overflowing on to the wall panels and the bath-mat. It was perfect.

He pulled on his jacket and opened the door.

'Edyth! Hurry, dearest!' The words were on the tip of his tongue but her arrival forestalled them. She came shrinking in, her blue dressing-gown strained round her thin body, her hair thrust into an unbecoming bathing cap.

'Oh, Ronald!' she said, staring at the display aghast. 'Won't it make an awful mess? Goodness! All over the floor!'

Her hesitation infuriated him.

'That won't matter,' he said savagely. 'You get in while the virtue of the foam is still there. Hurry. Meanwhile I'll go and change, myself. I'll give you ten minutes. Get straight in and lie down. It'll take some of the sallowness out of that skin of yours.'

He went out and paused, listening. She locked the door as he had known she would. The habit of a lifetime does not suddenly change with marriage. He heard the bolt slide home and forced himself to walk slowly down the passage. He gave her sixty seconds. Thirty to take off her things and thirty to hesitate on the brink of the rosy mass.

'How is it?' he shouted from the linen cupboard doorway.

She did not answer at once and the sweat broke out on his forehead. Then he heard her.

'I don't know yet. I'm only just in. It smells lovely.'

He did not wait for the final word, his hand wrapped in his handkerchief had found the main switch again.

'One, two ... three,' he said with horrible prosaicness and pulled it down.

From the wall socket behind him there was a single spluttering flare as the fuse went and then silence.

All round Ronald it was so quiet that he could hear the pulses in his own body, the faraway tick of a clock at the bottom of the stairs, the dreary buzzing of a fly imprisoned against the window glass and, from the garden next door, the drone of a mower as the heavy, fresh-faced man who had moved there, performed his weekly chore shaving the little green lawn. But from the bathroom there was no sound at all.

After a while he crept back along the passage and tapped at the door.

'Edyth?'

No. There was no response, no sound, nothing.

'Edyth?' he said again.

The silence was complete and, after a minute, he straightened his back and let out a deep sighing breath.

Almost at once he was keyed up again in preparing for the second phase. As he knew well, this next was the tricky period. The discovery of the body had got to be made but not too soon. He had made that mistake about Dorothy's 'accident' and had actually been asked by the local inspector why he had taken alarm so soon, but he had kept his head and the dangerous moment had

flickered past. This time he had made up his mind to make it half
an hour before he began to hammer loudly at the door, then to
shout for a neighbour and finally to force the lock. He had
planned to stroll out to buy an evening paper in the interim,
shouting his intention to do so to Edyth from the front step for
any passer-by to hear, but as he walked back along the landing
he knew there was something else he was going to do first.

Edyth's leather writing-case in which she kept all her private
papers was in the bottom of her soft-topped canvas hatbox. She
had really believed he had not known of its existence, he reflected
bitterly. It was locked, as he had discovered when he had at last
located it, and he had not prized the catch for fear of putting her
on her guard, but now there was nothing to stop him.

He went softly into the bedroom and opened the wardrobe
door. The case was exactly where he had last seen it, plump and
promising, and his hands closed over it gratefully. The catch was
a little more difficult than he had expected but he got it open at
last and the orderly contents of the leather box came into view.
At first sight it was all most satisfactory, far better than he had
anticipated. There were bundles of savings certificates, one or two
thick envelopes whose red seals suggested the offices of lawyers
and, on top, ready for the taking, one of those familiar blue books
which the Post Office issues to its savings bank clients.

He opened it with shaking fingers and fluttered through the
pages. Two thousand. The sum made him whistle. Two thousand
eight hundred and fifty. She must have paid in a decent dividend
there. Two thousand nine hundred. Then a drop as she had drawn
out a hundred pounds for her trousseau. Two thousand eight
hundred. He thought that was the final entry but on turning the
page saw that there was yet one other recorded transaction. It was
less than a week old. He remembered the book coming back
through the mail and how clever she had thought she had been in

smuggling the envelope out of sight. He glanced at the written words and figures idly at first but then as his heart jolted in sudden panic stared at them, his eyes prominent and glazed. She had taken almost all of it out. There it was in black and white: *September 4th Withdrawal Two thousand seven hundred and ninety-eight pounds.*

His first thought was that the money must still be there, in hundred-pound notes perhaps in one of the envelopes. He tore through them hastily, forgetting all caution in his anxiety. Papers, letters, certificates fell on the floor in confusion.

The envelope, addressed to himself, pulled him up short. It was new and freshly blotted, the name inscribed in Edyth's own unexpectedly firm hand. Ronald Torbay, Esqre.

He wrenched it open and smoothed the single sheet of bond paper within. The date, he noted in amazement, was only two days old.

Dear Ronald,

If you ever get this I am afraid it will prove a dreadful shock to you. For a long time I have been hoping that it might not be necessary to write it but now your behaviour has forced me to face some very unpleasant possibilities.

I am afraid, Ronald, that in some ways you are very old-fashioned. Had it not occurred to you that any homely middle-aged woman who has been swept into hasty marriage to a stranger must, unless she is a perfect idiot, be just a little suspicious and touchy on the subject of *baths*?

Your predecessor James Joseph Smith and his Brides* are not entirely forgotten, you know.

Frankly, I did not want to suspect you. For a long time I thought I was in love with you, but when you persuaded me to make my will on our wedding day I could not help wondering, and then as soon as you started fussing about the bathroom in this house I thought I had better do something about it rather quickly. I am old-fashioned too, so I went to the police.

Have you noticed that the people who have moved into the house next door have never tried to speak to you? We thought it best that I should merely talk to the woman over the garden wall, and it is she who has shown me the two cuttings from old provincial newspapers each about women who met with fatal accidents in bubble-baths soon after their marriages. In each case there was a press snapshot of the husband taken at the funeral. They are not very clear but as soon as I saw them I realized that it was my duty to agree to the course suggested to me by the inspector who has been looking for a man answering that description for three years, ever since the two photographs were brought to his notice by your poor second wife's brother.

What I am trying to say is this: if you should ever lose me, Ronald, out of the bathroom I mean, you will find that I have gone out over the roof and am sitting in my dressing-gown in the kitchen next door. I was a fool to marry you but not quite such a fool as you assumed. Women may be silly but they are not so stupid as they used to be. We are picking up the idea, Ronald.

Yours, Edyth

P.S. On re-reading this note I see that in my nervousness I have forgotten to mention that the new people next door are not a married couple but Detective Constable Batsford of the CID* and his assistant, Policewoman Richards. The police assure me that there cannot be sufficient evidence to convict you if you are not permitted to attempt the crime again. That is why I am forcing myself to be brave and to play my part, for I am very sorry for those other poor wives of yours, Ronald. They must have found you as fascinating as I did.

With his slit mouth twisted into an abominable 'O', Ronald Torbay raised haggard eyes from the letter.

The house was still quiet and even the whine of the mower in the next door garden had ceased. In the hush he heard a sudden clatter as the back door burst open and heavy footsteps raced through the hall and up the stairs towards him.

NOTES

Council (p93)
the local government office for the town or region, who would be responsible for maintaining the houses they owned

James Joseph Smith and his Brides (p98)
a well-known murderer who killed his wives in the bath

CID (p99)
the Criminal Investigation Department

DISCUSSION

1 Do you think the title of the story is an appropriate one? Was three, in fact, a lucky number? What other titles can you think of to suit the story?

2 What reasons can you give for the failure of Ronald's plan to kill Edyth? Was there a flaw in the method itself? Did Ronald omit to take some necessary precaution? Do you think he was outwitted by Edyth, or was it his own conceit that was the cause?

LANGUAGE FOCUS

1 Find these expressions in the story and rephrase them in your own words.

success was liable to go to a man's head (p89)
he did not dwell on the fact (p89)
the insurance had paid up without a murmur (p91)
He had an eye for stones (p91)
he ... had weathered the initial snub (p91)
she was ... as much at sea as a ship without a rudder (p91)
not to let her toes touch the ground (p91)
Two things signed her death warrant (p92)
he had kept his head (p96)
The envelope ... pulled him up short (p98)

2 Find all the descriptions in the story of Edyth's appearance and character. What are the contrasts between the impression suggested by her appearance and her character as revealed by later events? What

other ways can you think of to describe her character? Look again at her letter to Ronald. Which of these adjectives could describe the tone of the letter:

vindictive, triumphant, apologetic, regretful, matter-of-fact, angry, bitter, self-deprecating, sad, contemptuous, nervous, hysterical, threatening, friendly, generous?

ACTIVITIES

1 Write the newspaper report of the death of Ronald's first wife, Mary, including the flowery paragraph about 'the nearness of tragedy in the midst of joy'.

2 The story is told from Ronald's point of view. Look again at the last part of the story, from the moment when Edyth enters the bathroom, and rewrite the ending from her point of view, describing what she does and thinks. You might begin like this:

Edyth could see that her worry about the foam making a mess was infuriating Ronald. Savagely, he ordered her to get into the bath. When he went out, she quickly locked the door, and listened to him walking away down the passage. She knew she must wait for a few minutes in case he called out to her, but very slowly and carefully, she began to open the window . . .

3 Imagine that Ronald does succeed in murdering Edyth and continues with the discovery of the 'accident', with a neighbour present, as planned. Write his statement for the police, inventing the lies you think he might tell. For example, it was Edyth who insisted on having a heater in the bathroom, Edyth who was so fond of foam bubble-baths.

THE ADVENTURE OF
THE RETIRED COLOURMAN

THE AUTHOR

Sir Arthur Conan Doyle was born in 1859. He was so poor as a young doctor that he started writing to supplement his income. His first book, *A Study in Scarlet*, introduced the most famous detective in British fiction, Sherlock Holmes, expert in deduction and disguise, and his good-natured friend, Dr Watson. *The Adventures of Sherlock Holmes* were serialized in the Strand Magazine, and every episode was eagerly awaited by a large readership. Conan Doyle himself preferred the historical romances that he wrote, but the public could not have enough of his Sherlock Holmes stories. When in one story he killed Sherlock Holmes off, he was obliged by the public outcry to bring him back from the dead and continue writing about him. His stories not only describe methods of detection in great detail, but also the horror of the unknown, as in *The Hound of the Baskervilles*. He died in 1930.

THE STORY

In all classic detective stories nothing is quite as it seems. Sometimes it is not clear what crime, if any, has been committed. But the clues are always there, cunningly disguised or hidden. Of course, it often takes the sharp mind of a great detective to unravel the mystery.

Sherlock Holmes lies back in his deep armchair, his eyes apparently closed. He might even be asleep. Dr Watson, meanwhile, dutifully reports on his visit to a client's house, and after a time Holmes begins to show a gleam of interest. His questions become more penetrating, and more obscure. Dr Watson is puzzled.

'It's quite simple, my dear Watson,' says the great detective . . .

THE ADVENTURE OF
THE RETIRED COLOURMAN

Sherlock Holmes was in a melancholy and philosophic mood that morning. His alert practical nature was subject to such reactions.

'Did you see him?' he asked.

'You mean the old fellow who has just gone out?'

'Precisely.'

'Yes, I met him at the door.'

'What did you think of him?'

'A pathetic, futile, broken creature.'

'Exactly, Watson. Pathetic and futile. But is not all life pathetic and futile? Is not his story a microcosm of the whole? We reach. We grasp. And what is left in our hands at the end? A shadow. Or worse than a shadow – misery.'

'Is he one of your clients?'

'Well, I suppose I may call him so. He has been sent on by the Yard*. Just as medical men occasionally send their incurables to a quack. They argue that they can do nothing more, and that whatever happens the patient can be no worse than he is.'

'What is the matter?'

Holmes took a rather soiled card from the table. 'Josiah Amberley. He says he was junior partner of Brickfall and Amberley, who are manufacturers of artistic materials. You will see their names upon paint-boxes. He made his little pile, retired from business at the age of sixty-one, bought a house at Lewisham, and settled down to rest after a life of ceaseless grind. One would think his future was tolerably assured.'

'Yes, indeed.'

Holmes glanced over some notes which he had scribbled upon

the back of an envelope.

'Retired in 1896, Watson. Early in 1897 he married a woman twenty years younger than himself – a good-looking woman, too, if the photograph does not flatter. A competence*, a wife, leisure – it seemed a straight road which lay before him. And yet within two years he is, as you have seen, as broken and miserable a creature as crawls beneath the sun.'

'But what has happened?'

'The old story, Watson. A treacherous friend and a fickle wife. It would appear that Amberley has one hobby in life, and it is chess. Not far from him at Lewisham there lives a young doctor who is also a chess-player. I have noted his name as Dr Ray Ernest. Ernest was frequently in the house, and an intimacy between him and Mrs Amberley was a natural sequence, for you must admit that our unfortunate client has few outward graces, whatever his inner virtues may be. The couple went off together last week – destination untraced. What is more, the faithless spouse carried off the old man's deedbox as her personal luggage with a good part of his life's savings within. Can we find the lady? Can we save the money? A commonplace problem so far as it has developed, and yet a vital one for Josiah Amberley.'

'What will you do about it?'

'Well, the immediate question, my dear Watson, happens to be, What will *you* do? – if you will be good enough to understudy me. You know that I am preoccupied with this case of the two Coptic Patriarchs, which should come to a head today. I really have not time to go out to Lewisham, and yet evidence taken on the spot has a special value. The old fellow was quite insistent that I should go, but I explained my difficulty. He is prepared to meet a representative.'

'By all means,' I answered. 'I confess I don't see that I can be of much service, but I am willing to do my best.' And so it was

that on a summer afternoon I set forth to Lewisham, little
dreaming that within a week the affair in which I was engaging
would be the eager debate of all England.

It was late that evening before I returned to Baker Street and gave
an account of my mission. Holmes lay with his gaunt figure
stretched in his deep chair, his pipe curling forth slow wreaths of
acrid tobacco, while his eyelids drooped over his eyes so lazily
that he might almost have been asleep were it not that at any halt
or questionable passage of my narrative they half lifted, and two
grey eyes, as bright and keen as rapiers, transfixed me with their
searching glance.

'The Haven is the name of Mr Josiah Amberley's house,' I
explained. 'I think it would interest you, Holmes. It is like some
penurious patrician who has sunk into the company of his
inferiors. You know that particular quarter, the monotonous
brick streets, the weary suburban highways. Right in the middle
of them, a little island of ancient culture and comfort, lies this old
home, surrounded by a high sun-baked wall, mottled with lichens
and topped with moss, the sort of wall –'

'Cut out the poetry, Watson,' said Holmes severely. 'I note that
it was a high brick wall.'

'Exactly. I should not have known which was The Haven had
I not asked a lounger who was smoking in the street. I have reason
for mentioning him. He was a tall, dark, heavily-moustached,
rather military-looking man. He nodded an answer to my inquiry
and gave me a curiously questioning glance, which came back to
my memory a little later.

'I had hardly entered the gateway before I saw Mr Amberley
coming down the drive. I only had a glimpse of him this morning,
and he certainly gave me the impression of a strange creature, but
when I saw him in full light his appearance was even more

abnormal.'

'I have, of course, studied it, and yet I should be interested to have your impression,' said Holmes.

'He seemed to me like a man who was literally bowed down by care. His back was curved as though he carried a heavy burden. Yet he was not the weakling that I had at first imagined, for his shoulders and chest have the framework of a giant, though his figure tapers away into a pair of spindled legs.'

'Left shoe wrinkled, right one smooth.'

'I did not observe that.'

'No, you wouldn't. I spotted his artificial limb. But proceed.'

'I was struck by the snaky locks of grizzled hair which curled from under his old straw hat, and his face with its fierce, eager expression and the deeply-lined features.'

'Very good, Watson. What did he say?'

'He began pouring out the story of his grievances. We walked down the drive together, and of course I took a good look round. I have never seen a worse-kept place. The garden was all running to seed, giving me an impression of wild neglect in which the plants had been allowed to find the way of nature rather than of art. How any decent woman could have tolerated such a state of things, I don't know. The house, too, was slatternly to the last degree, but the poor man seemed himself to be aware of it and to be trying to remedy it, for a great pot of green paint stood in the centre of the hall and he was carrying a thick brush in his left hand. He had been working on the woodwork.

'He took me into his dingy sanctum, and we had a long chat. Of course, he was disappointed that you had not come yourself. "I hardly expected," he said, "that so humble an individual as myself, especially after my heavy financial loss, could obtain the complete attention of so famous a man as Mr Sherlock Holmes."

'I assured him that the financial question did not arise. "No, of course, it is art for art's sake with him," said he; "but even on the artistic side of crime he might have found something here to study. And human nature, Dr Watson – the black ingratitude of it all! When did I ever refuse one of her requests? Was ever a woman so pampered? And that young man – he might have been my own son. He had the run of my house. And yet see how they have treated me! Oh, Dr Watson, it is a dreadful, dreadful world!"

'That was the burden of his song for an hour or more. He had, it seems, no suspicion of an intrigue. They lived alone save for a woman who comes in by the day and leaves every evening at six. On that particular evening old Amberley, wishing to give his wife a treat, had taken two upper circle seats at the Haymarket Theatre. At the last moment she had complained of a headache and had refused to go. He had gone alone. There seemed to be no doubt about the fact, for he produced the unused ticket which he had taken for his wife.'

'That is remarkable – most remarkable,' said Holmes, whose interest in the case seemed to be rising. 'Pray continue, Watson. I find your narrative most interesting. Did you personally examine this ticket? You did not, perchance, take the number?'

'It so happens that I did,' I answered with some pride. 'It chanced to be my old school number, thirty-one, and so it stuck in my head.'

'Excellent, Watson! His seat, then, was either thirty or thirty-two.'

'Quite so,' I answered, with some mystification. 'And on B row.'

'That is most satisfactory. What else did he tell you?'

'He showed me his strong-room, as he called it. It really is a strong-room – like a bank – with iron door and shutter – burglar-proof, as he claimed. However, the woman seems to have had a duplicate key, and between them they had carried off some seven thousand pounds' worth of cash and securities.'

'Securities! How could they dispose of those?'

'He said that he had given the police a list and that he hoped they would be unsaleable. He had got back from the theatre about midnight, and found the place plundered, the door and window open and the fugitives gone. There was no letter or message, nor has he heard a word since. He at once gave the alarm to the police.'

Holmes brooded for some minutes.

'You say he was painting. What was he painting?'

'Well, he was painting the passage. But he had already painted the door and woodwork of this room I spoke of.'

'Does it strike you as a strange occupation in the circumstances?'

' "One must do something to ease an aching heart." That was his own explanation. It was eccentric, no doubt, but he is clearly an eccentric man. He tore up one of his wife's photographs in my presence – tore it up furiously in a tempest of passion. "I never wish to see her damned face again," he shrieked.'

'Anything more, Watson?'

'Yes, one thing which struck me more than anything else. I had driven to the Blackheath Station and had caught my train there, when just as it was starting I saw a man dart into the carriage next to my own. You know that I have a quick eye for faces, Holmes. It was undoubtedly the tall, dark man whom I had addressed in the street. I saw him once more at London Bridge, and then I lost him in the crowd. But I am convinced that he was following me.'

'No doubt! No doubt!' said Holmes. 'A tall, dark, heavily-moustached man, you say, with grey-tinted sunglasses?'

'Holmes, you are a wizard. I did not say so, but he *had* grey-tinted sun-glasses.'

'And a Masonic* tie-pin?'

'Holmes!'

'Quite simple, my dear Watson. But let us get down to what is practical. I must admit to you that the case, which seemed to me to be so absurdly simple as to be hardly worth my notice, is rapidly assuming a very different aspect. It is true that though in your mission you have missed everything of importance, yet even those things which have obtruded themselves upon your notice give rise to serious thought.'

'What have I missed?'

'Don't be hurt, my dear fellow. You know that I am quite impersonal. No one else would have done better. Some possibly not so well. But clearly you have missed some vital points. What is the opinion of the neighbours about this man Amberley and his wife? That surely is of importance. What of Dr Ernest? Was he the gay Lothario* one would expect? With your natural advantages, Watson, every lady is your helper and accomplice. What about the girl at the post office, or the wife of the greengrocer? I can picture you whispering soft nothings with the young lady at the "Blue Anchor"*, and receiving hard somethings in exchange. All this you have left undone.'

'It can still be done.'

'It has been done. Thanks to the telephone and the help of the Yard, I can usually get my essentials without leaving this room. As a matter of fact, my information confirms the man's story. He has the local repute of being a miser as well as a harsh and exacting husband. That he had a large sum of money in that strong-room of his is certain. So also is it that young Dr Ernest, an unmarried man, played chess with Amberley, and probably played the fool with his wife. All this seems plain sailing, and one would think that there was no more to be said – and yet! – and yet!'

'Where lies the difficulty?'

'In my imagination, perhaps. Well, leave it there, Watson. Let us escape from this weary workaday world by the side door of music. Carina sings tonight at the Albert Hall, and we still have time to dress, dine and enjoy.'

In the morning I was up betimes, but some toast crumbs and two empty egg-shells told me that my companion was earlier still. I found a scribbled note on the table.

DEAR WATSON,

There are one or two points of contact which I should wish to establish with Mr Josiah Amberley. When I have done so we can dismiss the case – or not. I would only ask you to be on hand about three o'clock, as I conceive it possible that I may want you.   S.H.

I saw nothing of Holmes all day, but at the hour named he returned, grave, preoccupied and aloof. At such times it was easier to leave him to himself.

'Has Amberley been here yet?'

'No.'

'Ah! I am expecting him.'

He was not disappointed, for presently the old fellow arrived with a very worried and puzzled expression upon his austere face.

'I've had a telegram, Mr Holmes. I can make nothing of it.' He handed it over, and Holmes read it aloud.

Come at once without fail. Can give you information as to your recent loss. – ELMAN. The Vicarage.

'Dispatched at two-ten from Little Purlington,' said Holmes. 'Little Purlington is in Essex, I believe, not far from Frinton. Well, of course you will start at once. This is evidently from a responsible person, the vicar of the place. Where is my Crockford*? Yes, here we have him. J.C. Elman, M.A., Living of Mossmoor cum Little Purlington. Look up the trains, Watson.'

'There is one at five-twenty from Liverpool Street.'

'Excellent. You had best go with him, Watson. He may need help or advice. Clearly we have come to a crisis in this affair.'

But our client seemed by no means eager to start.

'It's perfectly absurd, Mr Holmes,' he said. 'What can this man possibly know of what has occurred? It is waste of time and money.'

'He would not have telegraphed to you if he did not know something. Wire at once that you are coming.'

'I don't think I shall go.'

Holmes assumed his sternest aspect.

'It would make the worst possible impression both on the police and upon myself, Mr Amberley, if when so obvious a clue arose you should refuse to follow it up. We should feel that you were not really in earnest in this investigation.'

Our client seemed horrified at the suggestion.

'Why, of course I shall go if you look at it in that way,' said he. 'On the face of it, it seems absurd to suppose that this parson knows anything, but if you think –'

'I *do* think,' said Holmes, with emphasis, and so we were launched upon our journey. Holmes took me aside before we left the room and gave me one word of counsel which showed that he considered the matter to be of importance. 'Whatever you do, see that he really *does* go,' said he. 'Should he break away or return, get to the nearest telephone exchange and send the single word "Bolted". I will arrange here that it shall reach me wherever I am.'

Little Purlington is not an easy place to reach, for it is on a branch line. My remembrance of the journey is not a pleasant one, for the weather was hot, the train slow, and my companion sullen and silent, hardly talking at all, save to make an occasional sardonic remark as to the futility of our proceedings. When we at last reached the little station it was a two-mile drive before we came to the Vicarage, where a big, solemn, rather pompous clergyman received us in his study. Our telegram lay before him.

'Well, gentlemen,' he asked, 'what can I do for you?'

'We came,' I explained, 'in answer to your wire.'

'My wire! I sent no wire.'

'I mean the wire which you sent to Mr Josiah Amberley about his wife and his money.'

'If this is a joke, sir, it is a very questionable one,' said the vicar angrily. 'I have never heard of the gentleman you name, and I have not sent a wire to anyone.'

Our client and I looked at each other in amazement.

'Perhaps there is some mistake,' said I; 'are there perhaps two vicarages? Here is the wire itself, signed Elman, and dated from the Vicarage.'

'There is only one vicarage, sir, and only one vicar, and this wire is a scandalous forgery, the origin of which shall certainly be investigated by the police. Meanwhile, I can see no possible object in prolonging this interview.'

So Mr Amberley and I found ourselves on the road-side in what seemed to me to be the most primitive village in England. We made for the telegraph office, but it was already closed. There was a telephone, however, at the little 'Railway Arms', and by it I got into touch with Holmes, who shared in our amazement at the result of our journey.

'Most singular!' said the distant voice. 'Most remarkable! I much fear, my dear Watson, that there is no return train tonight. I have unwittingly condemned you to the horrors of a country inn. However, there is always Nature, Watson – Nature and Josiah Amberley – you can be in close commune with both.' I heard his dry chuckle as he turned away.

It was soon apparent to me that my companion's reputation as a miser was not undeserved. He had grumbled at the expense of the journey, had insisted upon travelling third-class, and was now clamorous in his objections to the hotel bill. Next morning, when we did at last arrive in London, it was hard to say which of us was in the worse humour.

'You had best take Baker Street as we pass,' said I. 'Mr Holmes may have some fresh instructions.'

'If they are not worth more than the last ones they are not of much use,' said Amberley, with a malevolent scowl. None the less, he kept me company. I had already warned Holmes by telegram of the hour of our arrival, but we found a message waiting that he was at Lewisham, and would expect us there. That was a surprise, but an even greater one was to find that he was not alone in the sitting-room of our client. A stern-looking, impassive man sat beside him, a dark man with grey-tinted glasses and a large Masonic pin projecting from his tie.

'This is my friend Mr Barker,' said Holmes. 'He has been interesting himself also in your business, Mr Josiah Amberley, though we have been working independently. But we have both the same question to ask you!'

Mr Amberley sat down heavily. He sensed impending danger. I read it in his straining eyes and his twitching features.

'What is the question, Mr Holmes?'

'Only this: What did you do with the bodies?'

The man sprang to his feet with a hoarse scream. He clawed into the air with his bony hands. His mouth was open and for the instant he looked like some horrible bird of prey. In a flash we got a glimpse of the real Josiah Amberley, a misshapen demon with a soul as distorted as his body. As he fell back into his chair he clapped his hand to his lips as if to stifle a cough. Holmes sprang at his throat like a tiger, and twisted his face towards the ground. A white pellet fell from between his gasping lips.

'No short cuts, Josiah Amberley. Things must be done decently and in order. What about it, Barker?'

'I have a cab at the door,' said our taciturn companion.

'It is only a few hundred yards to the station. We will go together. You can stay here, Watson. I shall be back within half an hour.'

The old colourman had the strength of a lion in that great trunk of his, but he was helpless in the hands of the two experienced man-handlers. Wriggling and twisting he was dragged to the waiting cab and I was left to my solitary vigil in the ill-omened house. In less time than he had named, however, Holmes was back, in company with a smart young police inspector.

'I've left Barker to look after the formalities,' said Holmes. 'You had not met Barker, Watson. He is my hated rival upon the Surrey shore. When you said a tall dark man it was not difficult for me to complete the picture. He has several good cases to his credit, has he not, Inspector?'

'He has certainly interfered several times,' the Inspector answered with reserve.

'His methods are irregular, no doubt, like my own. The irregulars are useful sometimes, you know. You, for example, with your compulsory warning about whatever he said being used against him, could never have bluffed this rascal into what is virtually a confession.'

'Perhaps not. But we get there all the same, Mr Holmes. Don't imagine that we had not formed our own views of this case, and that we would not have laid our hands on our man. You will excuse us for feeling sore when you jump in with methods which we cannot use, and so rob us of the credit.'

'There shall be no such robbery, MacKinnon. I assure you that I efface myself from now onwards, and as to Barker, he has done nothing save what I told him.'

The Inspector seemed considerably relieved.

'That is very handsome of you, Mr Holmes. Praise or blame can matter little to you, but it is very different to us when the newspapers begin to ask questions.'

'Quite so. But they are pretty sure to ask questions anyhow, so it would be as well to have answers. What will you say, for example, when the intelligent and enterprising reporter asks you what the exact points were which aroused your suspicion, and finally gave you a certain conviction as to the real facts?'

The Inspector looked puzzled.

'We don't seem to have got any real facts yet, Mr Holmes. You say that the prisoner, in the presence of three witnesses, practically confessed, by trying to commit suicide, that he had murdered his wife and her lover. What other facts have you?'

'Have you arranged for a search?'

'There are three constables on their way.'

'Then you will soon get the clearest fact of all. The bodies cannot be far away. Try the cellars and the garden. It should not take long to dig up the likely places. This house is older than the water-pipes. There must be a disused well somewhere. Try your luck there.'

'But how did you know of it, and how was it done?'

'I'll show you first how it was done, and then I will give the explanation which is due to you, and even more to my long-suffering friend here, who has been invaluable throughout. But, first, I would give you an insight into this man's mentality. It is a very unusual one – so much so that I think his destination is more likely to be Broadmoor* than the scaffold. He has, to a high degree, the sort of mind which one associates with the medieval Italian nature rather than with the modern Briton. He was a miserable miser who made his wife so wretched by his niggardly ways that she was a ready prey for any adventurer. Such a one came upon the scene in the person of this chess-playing doctor. Amberley excelled at chess – one mark, Watson, of a scheming mind. Like all misers, he was a jealous man, and his jealousy became a frantic mania. Rightly or wrongly, he suspected an intrigue. He determined to have his revenge, and he planned it with diabolical cleverness. Come here!'

Holmes led us along the passage with as much certainty as if he had lived in the house, and halted at the open door of the strong-room.

'Pooh! What an awful smell of paint!' cried the Inspector.

'That was our first clue,' said Holmes. 'You can thank Dr Watson's observation for that, though he failed to draw the inference. It set my foot upon the trail. Why should this man at such a time be filling his house with strong odours? Obviously, to cover some other smell which he wished to conceal – some guilty smell which would suggest suspicions. Then came the idea of a room such as you see here with the iron door and shutter – a hermetically sealed room. Put those two facts together, and whither do they lead? I could only determine that by examining the house myself. I was already certain that the case was serious, for I had examined the box-office chart at the Haymarket Theatre – another of Dr Watson's bull's-eyes – and ascertained that neither B thirty nor thirty-two of the upper circle had been occupied that night. Therefore, Amberley had not been to the theatre, and his alibi fell to the ground. He made a bad slip when he allowed my astute friend to notice the number of the seat taken for his wife. The question now arose how I might be able to examine the house. I sent an agent to the most impossible village I could think of, and summoned my man to it at such an hour that he could not possibly get back. To prevent any miscarriage, Dr Watson accompanied him. The good vicar's name I took, of course, out of my Crockford. Do I make it all clear to you?'

'It is masterly,' said the Inspector, in an awed voice.

'There being no fear of interruption I proceeded to burgle the house. Burglary has always been an alternative profession, had I cared to adopt it, and I have little doubt that I should have come to the front. Observe what I found. You see the gas-pipe along the skirting here. Very good. It rises in the angle of the wall, and there is a tap here in the corner. The pipe runs out into the strong-room, as you can see, and ends in that plastered rose in the centre of the ceiling, where it is concealed by the ornamentation. The end is wide open. At any moment by turning the outside tap the room could be flooded with gas. With door and shutter closed and the tap full on I would not give two minutes of conscious sensation to anyone shut up in that little chamber. By what devilish device he decoyed them there I do not know, but once inside the door they were at his mercy.'

The Inspector examined the pipe with interest. 'One of our officers mentioned the smell of gas,' said he, 'but, of course, the window and door were open then, and the paint – or some of it – was already about. He had begun the work of painting the day before, according to his story. But what next, Mr Holmes?'

'Well, then came an incident which was rather unexpected to myself. I was slipping through the pantry window in the early dawn when I felt a hand inside my collar, and a voice said: "Now, you rascal, what are you doing in there?" When I could twist my head round I looked into the tinted spectacles of my friend and rival, Mr Barker. It was a curious foregathering, and set us both smiling. It seems that he had been engaged by Dr Ray Ernest's family to make some investigations, and had come to the same conclusion as to foul play. He had watched the house for some days, and had spotted Dr Watson as one of the obviously suspicious characters who had called there. He could hardly arrest Watson, but when he saw a man actually climbing out of the pantry window there came a limit to his restraint. Of course, I told him how matters stood and we continued the case together.'

'Why him? Why not us?'

'Because it was in my mind to put that little test which answered so admirably. I fear you would not have gone so far.'

The Inspector smiled.

'Well, maybe not. I understand that I have your word, Mr

Holmes, that you step right out of the case now and that you turn all your results over to us.'

'Certainly, that is always my custom.'

'Well, in the name of the Force I thank you. It seems a clear case, as you put it, and there can't be much difficulty over the bodies.'

'I'll show you a grim little bit of evidence,' said Holmes, 'and I am sure Amberley himself never observed it. You'll get results, Inspector, by always putting yourself in the other fellow's place, and thinking what you would do yourself. It takes some imagination, but it pays. Now, we will suppose that you were shut up in this little room, had not two minutes to live, but wanted to get even with the fiend who was probably mocking at you from the other side of the door. What would you do?'

'Write a message.'

'Exactly. You would like to tell people how you died. No use writing on paper. That would be seen. If you wrote on the wall some eye might rest upon it. Now, look here! Just above the skirting is scribbled with a purple indelible pencil: "We we–" That's all.'

'What do you make of that?'

'Well, it's only a foot above the ground. The poor devil was on the floor and dying when he wrote it. He lost his senses before he could finish.'

'He was writing, "We were murdered."'

'That's how I read it. If you find an indelible pencil on the body –'

'We'll look out for it, you may be sure. But those securities? Clearly there was no robbery at all. And yet he *did* possess those bonds. We verified that.'

'You may be sure he has them hidden in a safe place. When the whole elopement had passed into history he would suddenly discover them, and announce that the guilty couple had relented and sent back the plunder or had dropped it on the way.'

'You certainly seem to have met every difficulty,' said the Inspector. 'Of course, he was bound to call us in, but why he should have gone to you I can't understand.'

'Pure swank!' Holmes answered. 'He felt so clever and so sure of himself that he imagined no one could touch him. He could say to any suspicious neighbour, "Look at the steps I have taken. I have consulted not only the police, but even Sherlock Holmes." '

The Inspector laughed.

'We must forgive you your "even", Mr Holmes,' said he; 'it's as workmanlike a job as I can remember.'

A couple of days later my friend tossed across to me a copy of the bi-weekly *North Surrey Observer*. Under a series of flaming headlines, which began with 'The Haven Horror' and ended with 'Brilliant Police Investigation', there was a packed column of print which gave the first consecutive account of the affair. The concluding paragraph is typical of the whole. It ran thus:

The remarkable acumen by which Inspector MacKinnon deduced from the smell of paint that some other smell, that of gas, for example, might be concealed; the bold deduction that the strong-room might also be the death-chamber, and the subsequent inquiry which led to the discovery of the bodies in a disused well, cleverly concealed by a dog-kennel, should live in the history of crime as a standing example of the intelligence of our professional detectives.

'Well, well, MacKinnon is a good fellow,' said Holmes, with a tolerant smile. 'You can file it in our archives, Watson. Some day the true story may be told.'

NOTES

the Yard (p105)

Scotland Yard, the headquarters of the London police force and the Criminal Investigation Department

a competence (p106)

an income, usually unearned, large enough to live on (now seldom used with this meaning)

Masonic (p110)

of the Freemasons, an international secret society which aims to offer mutual help and friendship among its members

the gay Lothario (p111)

a heartless seducer of women (Lothario was a character in an eighteenth-century play)

the Blue Anchor (p111)

a likely name for a local pub or inn

Crockford (p112)

the publisher of a directory which lists names and details of clergymen in Britain

Broadmoor (p117)

a special hospital where criminals who are judged to be insane are kept (instead of in a prison)

DISCUSSION

1 Holmes both praised and criticized Watson's attempts at detection. Can you describe Holmes's attitude towards Watson, giving as many examples as possible?

2 Describe the detection skills used by Holmes in this story. How are his methods 'irregular'; that is, what did he do that the police would be unable to do?

3 Did you find the solution of the mystery predictable? If so, did that lessen your appreciation of the story?

LANGUAGE FOCUS

1 Conan Doyle often uses rather formal, even elaborate, language. Find these sentences and phrases in the story, and then try to rephrase them

in as simple a way as possible. For example:

- *I would ask you to be on hand about three o'clock, as I conceive it possible that I may want you.* (p112)
  Please be here about three o'clock, as I may want you.
- *... You must admit that our unfortunate client has few outward graces, whatever his inner virtues may be.* (p106)
- *I hardly expected that so humble an individual as myself, especially after my heavy financial loss, could obtain the complete attention of so famous a man as Mr Sherlock Holmes.* (p108)
- *... the case, which seemed to me to be so absurdly simple as to be hardly worth my notice, is rapidly assuming a very different aspect.* (p110/111)
- *With your natural advantages, Watson, every lady is your helper and accomplice.* (p111)
- *It would make the worst possible impression both on the police and upon myself, Mr Amberley, if when so obvious a clue arose you should refuse to follow it up.* (p113)
- *It was soon apparent to me that my companion's reputation as a miser was not undeserved.* (p114)
- *Such a one came upon the scene in the person of this chess-playing doctor.* (p117)
- *There being no fear of interruption I proceeded to burgle the house.* (p118)

2   The conversations between Dr Watson and Mr Amberley on their journeys to and from Little Purlington are described in a few expressive phrases:

- *... an occasional sardonic remark as to the futility of our proceedings*
- *... grumbled at the expense*
- *... insisted upon travelling third-class*
- *... clamorous in his objections*

Think of one or two actual remarks that Amberley might have made, which would fit each of these descriptions.

ACTIVITIES

1   Imagine you are Mr Barker, and are furious' that the police should
    take the credit due to a private detective. Write another short article
    for the *North Surrey Observer*, exposing the police claim to take the
    credit as fraudulent, and describing how your astute friend and
    colleague, Sherlock Holmes, was the man who unravelled the mystery
    of the horrible Amberley murders. Invent a suitably eye-catching
    headline for your article.

2   This story contains detailed descriptions of the appearance and nature
    of some of the characters, but none, of course, of the narrator himself.
    What do you think Dr Watson looks like, and what clues to his
    personality do you get from the story? Write a description of his
    appearance and character, and then compare your ideas with those of
    other students. Are your impressions similar?

Sauce for the Goose

The Author

Patricia Highsmith was born in 1921 in Texas, and grew up in New York. She decided to become a writer at the age of sixteen. Her first book, *Strangers on a Train*, was filmed by Alfred Hitchcock, and since then she has written many widely praised novels and collections of short stories. Her books are psychological thrillers, which show us, in a horribly convincing way, the darker side of human nature. Her series of novels about the charming but psychopathic Tom Ripley are particularly famous. Among her best-known titles are *The Talented Mr Ripley*, *Ripley's Game*, *The Two Faces of January*, and *The Glass Cell*.

The Story

Jealousy, greed, revenge. In the relationship of marriage any of these emotions can be a motive for murder. When you also have a rich older man with an attractive, and much younger, wife, then the scene is apparently set. But although the ingredients may be similar to those in the previous story by Conan Doyle, the mixture here might turn out to be rather different.

Loren Amory is rich, balding, and forty-five. His charming wife Olivia is eleven years younger, and Loren knows only too well the reason for her current depression and tearfulness. He is a sensible man, but naturally he becomes anxious when his wife has several near-accidents around the house . . .

Sauce for the Goose*

The incident in the garage was the third near-catastrophe in the Amory household, and it put a horrible thought into Loren Amory's head: his darling wife Olivia was trying to kill herself.

Loren had pulled at a plastic clothesline dangling from a high shelf in the garage – his idea had been to tidy up, to coil the clothesline properly – and at that first tug an avalanche of suitcases, an old lawnmower, and a sewing machine weighing God-knows-how-much crashed down on the spot that he barely had time to leap from.

Loren walked slowly back to the house, his heart pounding at his awful discovery. He entered the kitchen and made his way to the stairs. Olivia was in bed, propped against pillows, a magazine in her lap. 'What was that terrible noise, dear?'

Loren cleared his throat and settled his black-rimmed glasses more firmly on his nose. 'A lot of stuff in the garage. I pulled just a little bit on a clothesline –' He explained what had happened.

She blinked calmly as if to say, 'Well, so what? Things like that do happen.'

'Have you been up to that shelf for anything lately?'

'Why, no. Why?'

'Because – well, everything was just poised to fall, darling.'

'Are you blaming me?' she asked in a small voice.

'Blaming your carelessness, yes. I arranged those suitcases up there and I'd never have put them so they'd fall at a mere touch. And I didn't put the sewing machine on top of the heap. Now, I'm not saying –'

'Blaming my carelessness,' she repeated, affronted.

He knelt quickly beside the bed. 'Darling, let's not hide things

any more. Last week there was the carpet sweeper on the cellar
stairs. And that ladder! You were going to climb it to knock down
that wasps' nest! What I'm getting at, darling, is that you *want*
something to happen to you, whether you realize it or not. You've
got to be more careful, Olivia – Oh, darling, please don't cry. I'm
trying to help you. I'm not criticizing.'

'I know, Loren. You're good. But my life – it doesn't seem worth
living any more, I suppose. I don't mean I'm *trying* to end my life,
but –'

'You're still thinking – of Stephen?' Loren hated the name and
hated saying it.

She took her hands down from her pinkened eyes. 'You made
me promise you not to think of him, so I haven't. I swear it, Loren.'

'Good, darling. That's my little girl.' He took her hands in his.
'What do you say to a cruise soon? Maybe in February? Myers
is coming back from the coast and he can take over for me for a
couple of weeks. What about Haiti or Bermuda?'

She seemed to think about it for a moment, but at last shook
her head and said she knew he was only doing it for her, not
because he really wanted to go. Loren remonstrated briefly, then
gave it up. If Olivia didn't take to an idea at once, she never took
to it. There had been one triumph – his convincing her that it
made sense not to see Stephen Castle for a period of three months.

Olivia had met Stephen Castle at a party given by one of
Loren's colleagues on the Stock Exchange*. Stephen was
thirty-five, was ten years younger than Loren and one year
older than Olivia, and Stephen was an actor. Loren had no
idea how Toohey, their host that evening, had met him, or
why he had invited him to a party at which every other man
was either in banking or on the Exchange; but there he'd been,
like an evil alien spirit, and he'd concentrated on Olivia the
entire evening, and she'd responded with her charming smiles

that had captured Loren in a single evening eight years ago.

Afterwards, when they were driving back to Old Greenwich, Olivia had said, 'It's such fun to talk to somebody who's not in the stock-market for a change! He told me he's rehearsing in a play now – *The Frequent Guest*. We've got to see it, Loren.'

They saw it. Stephen Castle was on for perhaps five minutes in Act One. They visited Stephen backstage, and Olivia invited him to a cocktail party they were giving the following weekend. He came, and spent that night in their guest room. In the next weeks Olivia drove her car into New York at least twice a week on shopping expeditions, but she made no secret of the fact she saw Stephen for lunch on those days and sometimes for cocktails too. At last she told Loren she was in love with Stephen and wanted a divorce.

Loren was speechless at first, even inclined to grant her a divorce by way of being sportsmanlike; but forty-eight hours after her announcement he came to what he considered his senses. By that time he had measured himself against his rival – not merely physically (Loren did not come off so well there, being no taller than Olivia, with a receding hairline and a small paunch) but morally and financially as well. In the last two categories he had it all over Stephen Castle, and modestly he pointed this out to Olivia.

'I'd never marry a man for his money,' she retorted.

'I didn't mean you married me for my money, dear. I just happened to have it. But what's Stephen Castle ever going to have? Nothing much, from what I can see of his acting. You're used to more than he can give you. And you've known him only six weeks. How can you be sure his love for you is going to last?'

That last thought made Olivia pause. She said she would see Stephen just once more – 'to talk it over'. She drove to New York one morning and did not return until midnight. It was a Sunday, when Stephen had no performance. Loren sat up waiting for her.

In tears Olivia told him that she and Stephen had come to an understanding. They would not see each other for a month, and if at the end of that time they did not feel the same way about each other, they would agree to forget the whole thing.

'But of course you'll feel the same,' Loren said. 'What's a month in the life of an adult? If you'd try it for three months –'

She looked at him through tears. 'Three months?'

'Against the eight years we've been married? Is that unfair? Our marriage deserves at least a three-month chance, too, doesn't it?'

'All right, it's a bargain. Three months. I'll call Stephen tomorrow and tell him. We won't see each other or telephone for three months.'

From that day Olivia had gone into a decline. She lost interest in gardening, in her bridge club, even in clothes. Her appetite fell off, though she did not lose much weight, perhaps because she was proportionately inactive. They had never had a servant. Olivia took pride in the fact that she had been a working girl, a saleswoman in the gift department of a large store in Manhattan, when Loren met her. She liked to say that she knew how to do things for herself. The big house in Old Greenwich was enough to keep any woman busy, though Loren had bought every conceivable labour-saving device. They also had a walk-in deep freeze, the size of a large closet, in the basement, so that their marketing was done less often than usual, and all food was delivered, anyway. Now that Olivia seemed low in energy, Loren suggested getting a maid, but Olivia refused.

Seven weeks went by, and Olivia kept her word about not seeing Stephen. But she was obviously so depressed, so ready to burst into tears, that Loren lived constantly on the brink of weakening and telling her that if she loved Stephen that much, she had a right to see him. Perhaps, Loren thought, Stephen Castle was feeling the same way, also counting off the weeks until he could see Olivia again. If so, Loren had already lost.

But it was hard for Loren to give Stephen credit for feeling anything. He was a lanky, rather stupid chap with oat-coloured hair, and Loren had never seen him without a sickly smile on his mouth – as if he were a human billboard, perpetually displaying what he must have thought was his most flattering expression.

Loren, a bachelor until at thirty-seven he married Olivia, often sighed in dismay at the ways of women. For instance, Olivia: if he had felt so strongly about another woman, he would have set about promptly to extricate himself from his marriage. But here was Olivia hanging on, in a way. What did she expect to gain from it, he wondered. Did she think, or hope, that her infatuation for Stephen might disappear? Or did she know unconsciously that her love for Stephen Castle was all fantasy, and that her present depression represented to her and to Loren a fitting period of mourning for a love she didn't have the courage to go out and take?

But the Saturday of the garage incident made Loren doubt that Olivia was indulging in fantasy. He did not want to admit that Olivia was attempting to take her own life, but logic compelled him to. He had read about such people. They were different from the accident-prone, who might live to die a natural death, whatever that was. The others were the suicide-prone, and into this category he was sure Olivia fell.

A perfect example was the ladder episode. Olivia had been on the fourth or fifth rung when Loren noticed the crack in the left side of the ladder, and she had been quite unconcerned, even when he pointed it out to her. If it hadn't been for her saying she suddenly felt a little dizzy looking up at the wasps' nest, he never would have started to do the chore himself, and therefore wouldn't have seen the crack.

Loren noticed in the newspaper that Stephen's play was closing, and it seemed to him that Olivia's gloom deepened. Now there were dark circles under her eyes. She claimed she could not fall asleep before dawn.

'Call him if you want to, darling,' Loren finally said. 'See him once again and find out if you both –'

'No, I made a promise to you. Three months, Loren. I'll keep my promise,' she said with a trembling lip.

Loren turned away from her, wretched and hating himself.

Olivia grew physically weaker. Once she stumbled coming down the stairs and barely caught herself on the banister. Loren suggested, not for the first time, that she see a doctor, but she refused to.

'The three months are nearly up, dear. I'll survive them,' she said, smiling sadly.

It was true. Only two more weeks remained until 15 March, the three months' deadline. The Ides of March*, Loren realized for the first time. A most ominous coincidence.

On Sunday afternoon Loren was looking over some office reports in his study when he heard a long scream, followed by a clattering crash. In an instant he was on his feet and running. It had come from the cellar, he thought, and if so, he knew what had happened. That damned carpet sweeper again!

'Olivia?'

From the dark cellar he heard a groan. Loren plunged down the steps. There was a little whirr of wheels, his feet flew up in front of him, and in the few seconds before his head smashed against the cement floor he understood everything: Olivia had not fallen down the cellar steps, she had only lured him here; all this time she had been trying to kill *him*, Loren Amory – and all for Stephen Castle.

'I was upstairs in bed reading,' Olivia told the police, her hands shaking as she clutched her dressing gown around her. 'I heard a terrible crash and then – I came down –' She gestured helplessly toward Loren's dead body.

The police took down what she told them and commiserated with her. People ought to be more careful, they said, about things like carpet sweepers on dark stairways. There were fatalities like this every day in the United States. Then the body was taken away, and on Tuesday Loren Amory was buried.

Olivia rang Stephen on Wednesday. She had been telephoning him every day except Saturdays and Sundays, but she had not rung him since the previous Friday. They had agreed that any weekday she did not call him at his apartment at 11 a.m. would be a signal that their mission had been accomplished. Also, Loren Amory had got quite a lot of space on the obituary page Monday. He had left nearly a million dollars to his widow, and houses in Florida, Connecticut and Maine.

'Dearest! You look so tired!' were Stephen's first words to her when they met in an out-of-the-way bar in New York on Wednesday.

'Nonsense! It's all make-up,' Olivia said gaily. 'And you an actor!' She laughed. 'I have to look properly gloomy for my neighbours, you know. And I'm never sure when I'll run into someone I know in New York.'

Stephen looked around him nervously, then said with his habitual smile, 'Darling Olivia, how soon can we be together?'

'Very soon,' she said promptly. 'Not up at the house, of course, but remember we talked about a cruise? Maybe Trinidad? I've got the money with me. I want you to buy the tickets.'

They took separate staterooms, and the local Connecticut paper, without a hint of suspicion, reported that Mrs Amory's voyage was for reasons of health.

Back in the United States in April, suntanned and looking much improved Olivia confessed to her friends that she had met someone she was 'interested in'. Her friends assured her that was normal, and that she shouldn't be alone for the rest of her life. The curious thing was that when Olivia invited Stephen to a dinner party at her house, none of her friends remembered him, though several had met him at that cocktail party a few months before. Stephen was much more sure of himself now, and he behaved like an angel, Olivia thought.

In August they were married. Stephen had been getting nibbles in the way of work, but nothing materialized. Olivia told him not to worry, that things would surely pick up after the summer. Stephen did not seem to worry very much, though he protested he ought to work, and said if necessary he would try for some television parts. He developed an interest in gardening, planted some young blue spruces, and generally made the place look alive again.

Olivia was delighted that Stephen liked the house, because she did. Neither of them ever referred to the cellar stairs, but they had a light switch put at the top landing, so that a similar thing could not occur again. Also, the carpet sweeper was kept in its proper place, in the broom closet in the kitchen.

They entertained more often than Olivia and Loren had done. Stephen had many friends in New York, and Olivia found them amusing. But Stephen, Olivia thought, was drinking just a little too much. At one party, when they were all out on the terrace, Stephen nearly fell over the parapet. Two of the guests had to grab him.

'Better watch out for yourself in this house, Steve,' said Parker Barnes, an actor friend of Stephen's. 'It just might be jinxed.'

'What d'ya mean?' Stephen asked. 'I don't believe that for a minute. I may be an actor, but I haven't got a single superstition.'

'Oh, so you're an actor, Mr Castle!' a woman's voice said out of the darkness.

After the guests had gone, Stephen asked Olivia to come out again on the terrace.

'Maybe the air'll clear my head,' Stephen said, smiling. 'Sorry I was tipsy tonight. There's old Orion. See him?' He put his arm around Olivia and drew her close. 'Brightest constellation in the heavens.'

'You're hurting me, Stephen! Not so –' Then she screamed and squirmed, fighting for her life.

'Damn you!' Stephen gasped, astounded at her strength.

She twisted away from him and was standing near the bedroom door, facing him now. 'You were going to push me over.'

'No! Good God, Olivia! – I lost my balance, that's all. I thought I was going over myself!'

'That's a fine thing to do, then, hold on to a woman and pull her over too.'

'I didn't realize. I'm drunk, darling. And I'm sorry.'

They lay as usual in the same bed that night, but both of them were only pretending to sleep. Until, for Olivia at least, just as she had used to tell Loren, sleep came around dawn.

The next day, casually and surreptitiously, each of them looked over the house from attic to cellar – Olivia with a view to protecting herself from possible death traps, Stephen with a view to setting them. He had already decided that the cellar steps offered the best possibility, in spite of the duplication, because he thought no one would believe anyone would dare to use the same means twice – if the intention was murder.

Olivia happened to be thinking the same thing.

The cellar steps had never before been so free of impediments or so well lighted. Neither of them took the initiative to turn the light out at night. Outwardly each professed love and faith in the other.

'I'm sorry I ever said such a thing to you, Stephen,' she

whispered in his ear as she embraced him. 'I was afraid on the terrace that night, that's all. When you said "Damn you" –'

'I know, angel. You *couldn't* have thought I meant to hurt you. I said "Damn you" just because you were there, and I thought I might be pulling you over.'

They talked about another cruise. They wanted to go to Europe next spring. But at meals they cautiously tasted every item of food before beginning to eat.

How could *I* have done anything to the food, Stephen thought to himself, since you never leave the kitchen while you're cooking it.

And Olivia: I don't put anything past you. There's only one direction you seem to be bright in, Stephen.

Her humiliation in having lost a lover was hidden by a dark resentment. She realized she had been victimized. The last bit of Stephen's charm had vanished. Yet now, Olivia thought, he was doing the best job of acting in his life – and a twenty-four-hour-a-day acting job at that. She congratulated herself that it did not fool her, and she weighed one plan against another, knowing that this 'accident' had to be even more convincing than the one that had freed her from Loren.

Stephen realized he was not in quite so awkward a position. Everyone who knew him and Olivia, even slightly, thought he adored her. An accident would be assumed to be just that, an accident, if he said so. He was now toying with the idea of the closet-sized deep freeze in the cellar. There was no inside handle on the door, and once in a while Olivia went into the farthest corner of the deep freeze to get steaks or frozen asparagus. But would she dare to go into it, now that her suspicions were aroused, if he happened to be in the cellar at the same time? He doubted it.

While Olivia was breakfasting in bed one morning – she had

taken to her own bedroom again, and Stephen brought her breakfast as Loren had always done – Stephen experimented with the door of the deep freeze. If it so much as touched a solid object in swinging open, he discovered, it would slowly but surely swing shut on its rebound. There, was no solid object near the door now, and on the contrary the door was intended to be swung fully open, so that a catch on the outside of the door would lock in a grip set in the wall for just that purpose, and thus keep the door open. Olivia, he had noticed, always swung the door wide when she went in, and it latched on to the wall automatically. But if he put something in its way, even the corner of the box of kindling wood, the door would strike it and swing shut again, before Olivia had time to realize what had happened.

However, that particular moment did not seem the right one to put the kindling box in position, so Stephen did not set his trap. Olivia had said something about their going out to a restaurant tonight. She would not be taking anything out to thaw today.

They took a little walk at three in the afternoon – through the woods behind the house, then back home again – and they almost started holding hands, in a mutually distasteful and insulting pretence of affection; but their fingers only brushed and separated.

'A cup of tea would taste good, wouldn't it, darling?' said Olivia.

'Um-m.' He smiled. Poison in the tea? Poison in the cookies? She'd made them herself that morning.

He remembered how they had plotted Loren's sad demise – her tender whispers of murder over their luncheons, her infinite patience as the weeks went by and plan after plan failed. It was he who had suggested the carpet sweeper on the cellar steps and the lure of a scream from her. What could *her* bird-brain ever plan?

Shortly after their tea – everything had tasted fine – Stephen strolled out of the living room as if with no special purpose. He felt compelled to try out the kindling box again to see if it could really be depended on. He felt inspired, too, to set the trap now and leave it. The light at the head of the cellar stairs was on. He went carefully down the steps.

He listened for a moment to see if Olivia was possibly following him. Then he pulled the kindling box into position, not parallel to the front of the deep freeze, of course, but a little to one side, as if someone had dragged it out of the shadow to see into it better and left it there. He opened the deep-freeze door with exactly the speed and force Olivia might use, flinging the door from him as he stepped in with one foot, his right hand outstretched to catch the door on the rebound. But the foot that bore his weight slid several inches forward just as the door bumped against the kindling box.

Stephen was down on his right knee, his left leg straight out in front of him, and behind him the door shut. He got to his feet instantly and faced the closed door wide-eyed. It was dark, and he groped for the auxiliary switch to the left of the door, which put a light on at the back of the deep freeze.

How had it happened? The damned glaze of frost on the floor! But it wasn't only the frost, he saw. What he had slipped on was a little piece of suet that he now saw in the middle of the floor, at the end of the greasy streak his slide had made.

Stephen stared at the suet neutrally, blankly, for an instant, then faced the door again, pushed it, felt along its firm rubber-sealed crack. He could call Olivia, of course. Eventually she'd hear him, or at least *miss* him, before he had time to freeze. She'd come down to the cellar, and she'd be able to hear him there even if she couldn't hear him in the living room. Then she'd open the door, of course.

He smiled weakly, and tried to convince himself she *would* open the door.

'Olivia? – *Olivia*! I'm down in the *cellar*!'

It was nearly a half hour later when Olivia called to Stephen to ask him which restaurant he preferred, a matter that would influence what she wore. She looked for him in his bedroom, in the library, on the terrace, and finally called out the front door, thinking he might be somewhere on the lawn.

At last she tried the cellar.

By this time, hunched in his tweed jacket, his arms crossed, Stephen was walking up and down in the deep freeze, giving out distress signals at intervals of thirty seconds and using the rest of his breath to blow into his shirt in an effort to warm himself. Olivia was just about to leave the cellar when she heard her name called faintly.

'Stephen?– Stephen, where are you?'

'In the deep freeze!' he called as loudly as he could.

Olivia looked at the deep freeze with an incredulous smile.

'Open it, can't you? I'm in the *deep freeze*!' came his muffled voice.

Olivia threw her head back and laughed, not even caring if Stephen heard her. Then still laughing so hard that she had to bend over, she climbed the cellar stairs.

What amused her was that she had thought of the deep freeze as a fine place to dispose of Stephen, but she hadn't worked out how to get him into it. His being there now, she realized, was owing to some funny accident – maybe he'd been trying to set a trap for her. It was all too comical. And lucky!

Or, maybe, she thought cagily, his intention even now was to trick her into opening the deep-freeze door, then to yank her inside and close the door on her. She was certainly not going to let *that* happen!

Olivia took her car and drove nearly twenty miles northward, had a sandwich at a roadside café, then went to a movie. When she got home at midnight she found she had not the courage to call 'Stephen' to the deep freeze, or even to go down to the cellar. She wasn't sure he'd be dead by now, and even if he were silent it might mean he was only pretending to be dead or unconscious.

But tomorrow, she thought, there wouldn't be any doubt he'd be dead. The very lack of air, for one thing, ought to finish him by that time.

She went to bed and assured herself a night's sleep with a light sedative. She would have a strenuous day tomorrow. Her story of the mild quarrel with Stephen – over which restaurant they'd go to, nothing more – and his storming out of the living room to take a walk, she thought, would have to be very convincing.

At ten the next morning, after orange juice and coffee, Olivia felt ready for her role of the horrified, grief-stricken widow. After all, she told herself, she had practised the role – it would be the second time she had played the part. She decided to face the police in her dressing gown, as before.

To be quite natural about the whole thing she went down to the cellar to make the 'discovery' before she called the police.

'Stephen? Stephen?' she called out with confidence.

No answer.

She opened the deep freeze with apprehension, gasped at the curled-up, frost-covered figure on the floor, then walked the few feet toward him – aware that her footprints on the floor would be visible to corroborate her story that she had come in to try to revive Stephen.

Ka-*bloom* went the door – as if someone standing outside had given it a good hard push.

Now Olivia gasped in earnest, and her mouth stayed open. She'd flung the door wide. It should have latched on to the outside wall.

'Hello! Is anybody out there? Open this door, please! At once!'

But she knew there was no one out there. It was just some damnable accident. Maybe an accident that Stephen had arranged.

She looked at his face. His eyes were open, and on his white lips was his familiar little smile, triumphant now, and utterly nasty. Olivia did not look at him again. She drew her flimsy dressing gown as closely about her as she could and began to yell.

'Help! Someone! – *police*!'

She kept it up for what seemed like hours, until she grew hoarse and until she did not really feel very cold any more, only a little sleepy.

Notes

sauce for the goose (title)
part of the saying 'what's sauce for the goose is sauce for the gander':
what is suitable for one person (e.g. a wife) must also be suitable for
another (e.g. a husband)

the Stock Exchange (p127)
a financial centre where stocks and shares are bought and sold

the Ides of March (p131)
15th March, according to the ancient Roman calendar, which was the
day Julius Caesar was murdered (famous from the warning given in
Shakespeare's play *Julius Caesar*)

Discussion

1   Why do you think the author chose this title for the story? Think of
    some other titles and decide if they are less, or more, appropriate than
    the original one.

2   There are various motives for murder in this story. Can you explain
    why Olivia arranged to kill Loren, why Stephen planned to kill Olivia,
    and why Olivia wanted to kill Stephen?

3   How and why did Stephen and Olivia die in the end? Did the ending
    surprise you? Did you find it shocking, or satisfying?

4   Do you feel sympathy for anyone in the story? Why, or why not?

Language Focus

1   Look through the story and find these expressions, then rephrase them
    in your own words, keeping the sense of the original sentence.

    what I'm getting at (p127)
    he can take over for me (p127)
    then gave it up (p127)
    didn't take to an idea (p127)
    Loren did not come off so well there (p128)
    talk it over (p128)
    her appetite fell off (p129)

he would have set about promptly (p130)
here was Olivia hanging on (p130)
I'll run into someone (p132)
watch out for yourself (p133)
I don't put anything past you (p135)
she had taken to her own bedroom again (p136)
giving out distress signals (p138)
she kept it up (p140)

2   The story is told in a simple, matter-of-fact style. For example, look
    at the moments of crisis for each of the three main characters:

    - *... all this time she had been trying to kill him, Loren Amory –
      and all for Stephen Castle.*
    - *[Stephen] smiled weakly, and tried to convince himself she would
      open the door.*
    - *But she knew there was no one out there. It was just some
      damnable accident ...*

    What effect does this deliberate understatement have? Try rewriting
    each of the incidents, using adjectives and imagery to describe the
    emotions (e.g. *in those few seconds the terrible truth burst upon his
    mind like a bomb exploding ...*). Then compare your versions with
    the original. Does either version make you feel more sympathetic
    towards the characters?

ACTIVITIES

1   When the two frozen bodies are eventually discovered in the deep
    freeze, the police are completely mystified. Were they both accidental
    deaths? Was it one murder and one accident? A double murder? A
    suicide attempt? Was Loren Amory's death perhaps not just a simple
    accident? Write three short reports for different newspapers, each
    report giving a completely different theory as to the explanation of
    the tragedy.

2   Imagine that Olivia did not lock herself in the deep freeze, and write a
    new ending for the story. Do the police believe her account of Stephen's
    death? Do her friends get suspicious? How does her life continue?
    Does she marry again, and murder again? Does she ever feel remorse?

QUESTIONS FOR DISCUSSION OR WRITING

1   Which of these eight stories did you like, or dislike, most? Why?

2   Look again at these stories and list the reasons why the murders were committed. Do any of the murderers have similar motives? Do you sympathize with any of them?

3   If you were a defence lawyer, which of the murderers in these stories would you choose to defend at their trial? The actual murder is not disputed, but you want to get the minimum sentence for your client. Prepare a speech for your chosen murderer's defence, and think of witnesses you might call to support your case.

4   'There is no such thing as a moral or an immoral book. Books are well written, or badly written. That is all.' (Oscar Wilde, *The Picture of Dorian Gray*) Do you agree with this statement? Do you think that crime stories about murderers who escape punishment are immoral? Should criminals in fiction always be punished? Which of the murderers in these stories are not brought to justice? Are other kinds of punishment inflicted on them?

5   Crime and murder stories, whether told in novels and short stories, or in television plays and films, are always popular. Why do you think this is so? P.D. James, a very famous modern writer of crime novels, has offered an explanation for this. Detective stories continue to be popular, she says, because 'in an age when murder is so often random, the crime novel is a comforting form – it reassures us of the sanctity of life (if you get violently killed, someone will care) and of the fact that we live in a comprehensible, rational world, a world in which human authority, and human skill and integrity (the detective, the police), can put things to rights'.

Do you agree with this explanation? What is your own opinion? Are crime novels escapist fantasies, a long way from 'real' life? Are they told just for entertainment, or do they tell us something about human nature?

What other kinds, or genres, of stories can you think of? Make a list, e.g. love, war, ghost, science fiction, adventure, and so on. Do you find one genre more interesting or more enjoyable than others? If so, which one, and why?

6 Make a plan for a story about the 'perfect' murder. Invent a group of characters, including a murderer and a victim, and devise a murder plan that would baffle the sharp mind of even a Miss Marple or a Sherlock Holmes. Remember that the murderer must have

   a) motive
   b) means
   c) opportunity.

Make sure that your murderer has a cast-iron alibi, and that plenty of suspicion will fall on the other characters.